SCHOLASTIC

ACTIVE English 8

Coursebook

Name: ______________________________

Class: ______________________________

Text Credits

Sampurna Chattarji for *Yogurt and Cinnamon Dessert with Rose Geraniums and Peach* from *The Fried Frog and Other Funny Foodie Feisty Poems* (Scholastic India: 2009); *Mr Khan's Shop* from *Here Comes the Poetry Man* by Fred Sedgwick (Salt Publishing, 2011); *Boy* by Roald Dahl (Jonathan Cape Ltd & Penguin Books Ltd; pp. 54, 55, 58, 60); *Eyewitness Guide: Climate Change* by John Woodward (Dorling Kindersley, 2008). Copyright © 2008 Dorling Kindersley Limited. Reproduced by permission of Dorling Kindersley Ltd; *Paper* by Catherine Lim from *Little Ironies: Stories of Singapore*, (Heinemann Educational Books (Asia) Ltd, 1978); Scharada Dubey for *J.K. Rowling* from *The Best Days of My Life* (Scholastic India: 2008); *The Adventures of Tom Sawyer* by Mark Twain (American Publishing Company, 1876); Sharada Bhanu, Padma Malini Raghavan and Padma Seshadri for *Two Myths About Fire* from *103 Myths, Legends, Fables and Stuff* (Scholastic India: 2008); *Heaven and Earth and Man* from *Tales of China* retold by Cyril Birch (OUP, 2000; copyright © Cyril Birch 1961, reprinted by permission of Oxford University Press); *Healthy Eating for Teens* from www.nutrition.com.sg.

Photo credits

Wikimedia
P8 © Gran; P8 © Silar; P8 © Kim Scarborough; P8 © Mariuszjbie; P16 © Hartmut Inerle; P21 © Kirti Poddar ; P22 © Scott Dexter; P25 © Stu Spivack; P34 © Peter Gamble; P35 © Ansgar Walk; P35 © Brocken Inaglory; P37 © Alan D. Wilson; P49 © Kim Hansen; P50 © Hitesh vip; P56 © Stefan Kühn; P70 © Tony Atkin; P70©Rufustelestrat; P78 © Shazz; P82 © Elroy Serrao; P91 © Steven Hill; P132 © Allea78; P137 © Karen; P138 © USAID Bangladesh; P149 © James Gathany; P155 © Alpha.

Every effort has been made to trace the copyright holders of material used in this book. If any copyright holder has been overlooked, we will make any necessary arrangements at the first opportunity.

First edition 2012
Reprinted 2012, 2014 (twice), 2015 (twice), 2016, 2017, 2018, 2019, 2020, 2022, 2023, 2026

ISBN-978-81-8477-738-3

Printed in India at Saurabh Printers Pvt. Ltd.

Preface

The creators of ACTIVE **English** believe that literacy acquisition is dependent on the integrated teaching of reading, writing, listening and speaking skills, and the engagement of students. This integrated approach to learning and literacy development is advocated through a systematic and consistent instructional design and scope and sequence.

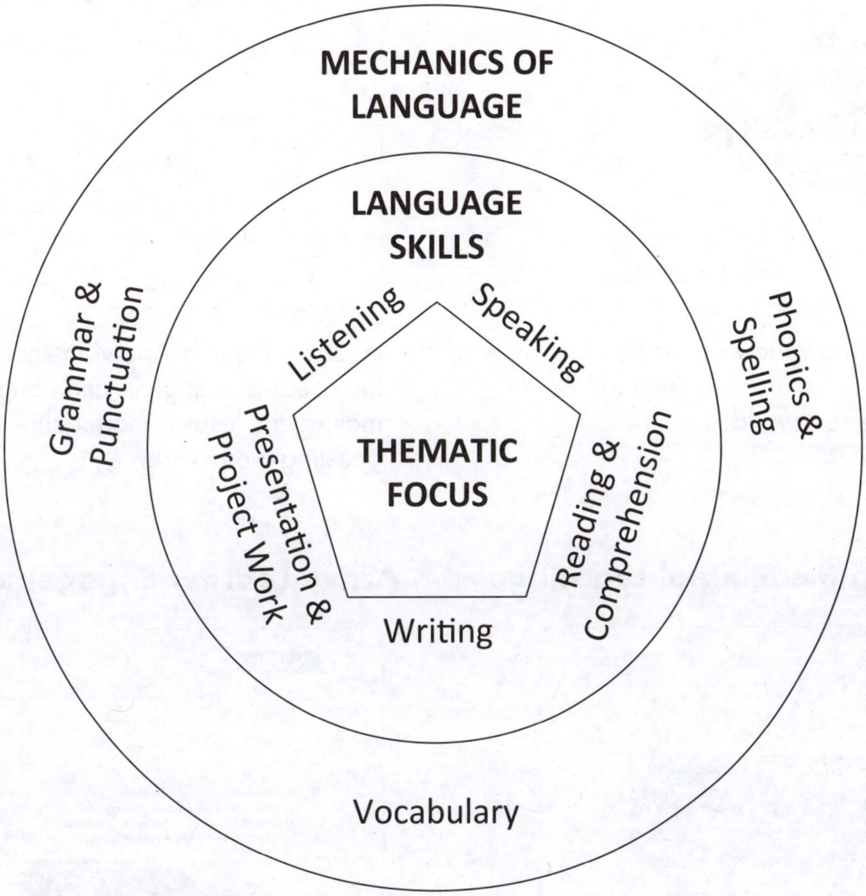

Each unit of the Coursebook has a thematic focus through which different language skills are meaningfully taught. Equal emphasis is given to each skill, enabling students to connect, transfer and build upon different skills.

Clear explanations and numerous examples give students a strong understanding of the mechanics of language and lay a strong foundation for good English.

As students progress through the levels, language skills are systematically taught at increasing levels of difficulty, allowing them to build upon small successes and reinforce the mechanics of language.

 ISBN-978-81-8477-738-3

Authentic and Varied Text Types

1 Yogurt and Cinnamon Dessert with Rose Geraniums and Peach

Read the following poem by Sampurna Chattarji.

1 Was her name Martha, or Marsha,
the one with the enchantress
hands?
A little eager, a little shy,
I walked into her kitchen that first morning
towards the smell of coffee and muffins.
"Blueberry!" she said, conspiratorially.
"Heaven," I said, one large bite
and two quick sips later. "Heaven on earth."

Authentic texts in a variety of text types engage students and prepare them for language in the real world.

Effective Instructional Design

Grammar

We use the **past continuous tense** to refer to actions that were ongoing at a certain point in the past. See the following examples.

Cadbury's **were using** some of the greatest chocolate-bar experts in the world to test out their new inventions.

I **was looking** for a plot for my second book.

We use the **future tense** when talking about future actions as shown in the example below.

I **will create** a new recipe for their anniversary.

We use the **future continuous tense** when talking about things that will be ongoing at a certain point in the future. See the following example.

I **will be creating** a new recipe for their anniversary.

A. Complete the sentences below using your own ideas.

1. So many delicious smells were wafting...
2. Inside the lab he was inventing...
3. They were creating...
4. We were having...
5. Nobody was walking...

A 'Show-Explain-Apply' methodology meets the needs of first generation English learners, making the lessons more achievable and boosting motivation.

Relevant and Meaningful Learning

Vocabulary

There are many words in the English language that are from other languages. These are called **loanwords**.

Here is a list of loanwords and the country of their origin. You may be surprised!

Loanword	Country and language of origin
poodle	Germany
smuggle	Germany/Holland
tea	Malay
bonsai	Japan
geranium	Greece
kiosk	Persian
graffiti	Italian
bazaar	Persian

All language skills are meaningfully taught in the context of a theme, connecting the learning to real life and increasing learning enjoyment.

Active Learner Engagement

Activity

A. Collect some data and facts on traffic in the following cities.

1. Mumbai
2. London
3. Beijing

B. You can decide on the kind of facts, information and data to be included. (For example, the number of vehicles travelling through the city over a given period, speed limits, traffic offences, road accidents, traffic improvements.)

C. Choose a way of presenting your data. Some suggestions are listed below.

1. a fact file
2. a table
3. a timeline (if you are presenting information over a period of time)
4. a combination of presentations

Activities throughout the units encourage students to actively participate and learn, improving retention and increasing the interaction between teacher and students.

 ISBN-978-81-8477-738-3

Ongoing and Accurate Assessment

Reading Comprehension

A. Answer the following questions.

Level 1

1. Scan parts I and II of the poem to find out information.
   - Where does the Lady of Shalott live?
   - What line in the first verse describes Camelot?
   - Mention three things one notices in the journey down to the Camelot in verse 3 of Part I?
   - When could the curse on the Lady of Shalott take effect?
   - What (in general) moves through the mirror that hangs in front of the Lady of Shalott?

Level 2

2. Who do you think the Lady of Shalott is? Look for evidence in the text to support your comments.
3. How does Sir Lancelot affect the Lady of Shalott?
4. How does the curse affect the Lady of Shalott?

B. Read the following note on metre in poetry and answer the questions.

Metre is the pattern of rhythm in verse and is referred to when discussing regular repeating patterns in poetry. It is the pattern of stressed and unstressed syllables.

/ = stressed

u = unstressed

66 Theme 3: Cautionary Tales

Speaking

Work in small groups (no more than four) to discuss the following questions.

1. In what way do humans always affect the environment and wildlife? Write your notes in the boxes.

Animal	Human action	Effect

2. How can we successfully cohabit with wildlife?

   Appoint a recorder to note the points and a reporter to report your discussion to another group.

Writing

Write an account about animals that are at risk of extinction.

44 Theme 2: The Environment

Ongoing assessment throughout and end-of-lesson evaluation allow accurate assessment of students' understanding.

Diversity of Contexts

5 The Lady of Shalott

Read the following poem by Alfred Lord Tennyson.

Part I

1 On either side the river lie
Long fields of barley and of rye,
That clothe the **wold** and meet the sky;
And thro' the field the road runs by
To many-tower'd Camelot;
And up and down the people go,
Gazing where the lilies blow
Round an island there below,
The island of Shalott.

2 Willows whiten, **aspens** quiver,
Little breezes dusk and shiver
Thro' the wave that runs for ever
By the island in the river
Flowing down to Camelot.
Four gray walls, and four gray towers,
Overlook a space of flowers,
And the silent isle **imbowers**
The Lady of Shalott.

3 By the margin, willow veil'd,
Slide the heavy barges trail'd
By slow horses; and unhail'd
The **shallop** flitteth silken-sail'd
Skimming down to Camelot:

wold: upland
aspens: type of poplar
imbowers: surrounds
shallop: shallow water boat

60 Theme 3: Cautionary Tales

12 Healthy Eating for Teens

Read the following passage.

1 Eating well is often hard for teens. Hanging around with friends, frequenting fast food outlets and snacking can lead to excessive intake of fat, sugar and calories and insufficient intake of important vitamins and minerals. Adolescence is a time of increased nutrient needs. During the rapid growth of puberty, the body has increased need for calories and key nutrients including protein, calcium, iron, folate and zinc. Iron and calcium are particularly important nutrients for your body during adolescence.

2 Iron helps your blood carry oxygen to all your muscles. It helps your brain function and your immune system fight disease. Choosing iron-rich food sources can help keep your body working optimally.

3 Your body will actually absorb more calcium from the foods you eat during puberty. The increased need for skeletal growth signals your body to "grab" all the calcium it can. The problem is most adolescents simply are not eating enough calcium-rich food to meet their needs. If you do not meet your calcium needs during this critical time when your bones are growing, you may end up with weaker bones that are more prone to fractures.

4 Experts estimate that for every 5 per cent increase in adolescent bone mass, there is a 40 per cent decrease in the risk of bone fractures later in life. There is a limited time window to deposit calcium into bone. Bones grow and incorporate calcium rapidly during teen years. By the time you reach your early twenties, however, calcium is no longer added to bone. Worse yet, when you get a little older, you actually start losing calcium from your bones. Currently most teen girls are getting far less than the recommended 700 milligrams of calcium per day. So, reach for foods rich in calcium now.

Unit 12: Healthy Eating for Teens 149

Familiar contexts provide relevance while international contexts broaden students' perspectives and prepare them to take the global stage.

We hope that all students will have fun in becoming active participants in their own learning and they will enjoy every success in the learning of English!

 ISBN-978-81-8477-738-3

Table of Contents

 ISBN-978-81-8477-738-3

Grammar/ Punctuation	Listening	Speaking	Writing	Activity
Imperatives	Listen to text on farming	Present a poem on food	Write a free-verse poem about food	Write a recipe for a dessert
Past continuous tense, future tense, future continuous tense	Listen to text on India's economic miracle	Present solutions to lessen traffic problems	Write an account about how other cities deal with traffic problems	Collect data on traffic and present it using a graphic organiser
Punctuation in a dialogue	Listen to text on human impact on the natural environment	Discuss the human impact on the environment and wildlife	Write an account about animals that are at risk of extinction	Carry out an investigation on the depictions of the polar bear in different forms
Modal verbs	Listen to text on nuclear energy	Discuss nuclear energy as an alternative energy source	Write an account about climate change and renewable energy	Find out how climate change is affecting various natural ecosystems
Hyphen and compound words	Listen to the verse	Discuss the poem *The Lady of Shalott*	Write a narrative poem	Produce a display on *The Lady of Shalott* and an Indian poem/legend
Adverbial phrases	Listen to further excerpt from *Paper*	Discuss what might happen in *Paper*	Compare and contrast what the characters in *Paper* value	Write a description from different points of view
Noun phrases	Listen to text on J. K. Rowling	Present a talk about who or what has influenced your ideas and behaviour	Write a short autobiography	Role-play an interview
Quotations	Listen to text about Mark Twain	Discuss the similarities and differences between Tom Sawyer and the children of today	Write a commentary on how Aunt Polly feels about Tom Sawyer	Create you own mischievous child character
Verb agreement	Listen to text on myths	Present a talk about the details given in *Two Myths About Fire*	Write your own myth	Use graphic organisers to present information about myths
Simple, compound and complex sentences	Listen to the resolution of *Ancient Myths*	Present a myth	Use the Fretag's pyramid to plan a story	Review the story plans in the 'Writing' section
Homographs	Listen to text on mobile health workers	Present a talk about mobile health workers	Write an article on a health-related topic	Create a leaflet about good hygiene
Gerunds	Listen to text on spices	Present a talk about healthy food and spices	Produce a diagram about spices and write a healthy recipe	Create a leaflet about healthy eating

 ISBN-978-81-8477-738-3

Theme 1

Food

Beetroot salad

Pancakes

Ravioli

Cabbage soup

Study the pictures and discuss the following questions with a partner.

1. What are the kinds of food that are depicted in the above pictures?
2. Can you guess the main ingredients in each dish?
3. Try to guess the name of the country these dishes belong to.
4. What provides a balanced diet? Also, write the ingredients of a meal that provides a balanced diet.

 ISBN-978-81-8477-738-3

1 Yogurt and Cinnamon Dessert with Rose Geraniums and Peach

Read the following poem by Sampurna Chattarji.

Was her name Martha, or Marsha,
the one with the enchantress
hands?
A little eager, a little shy,
I walked into her kitchen that first morning
towards the smell of coffee and muffins.
"Blueberry!" she said, conspiratorially.
"Heaven," I said, one large bite
and two quick sips later. "Heaven on earth."

 ISBN-978-81-8477-738-3

2 I counted them greedily,
three breakfasts, two dinners,
each outdoing the other.
Crisp bacon wrapped around soft seedless dates,
dips with cheese and herbs.
Served course-by-course, light pastas,
the right wine, voices reverential as we ate.
"*You'll* like this," she said the last evening,
knowing by then where I came from,
"It's **Yogurt** and **Cinnamon** Dessert
with Rose Geraniums and Peach."

3 I picked up a plate, and the first spoonful
Conjured up a taste I thought
I had forgotten, curd steamed with sugar
And cinnamon, a treat my mother made.
"The rose geraniums are an Irish thing,"
She said, "I picked that up in Ireland."
Her cheeks were flushed. Was it my delight?
Or was it the heat from her oven?
India America Ireland. Cinnamon yogurt and peach.
"You're astonishing, Martha," I said, for Martha it was,
And I was happy and close, so close, to tears.

---

yogurt: a custard-like food with a tart flavour, prepared from milk curdled by bacteria
cinnamon: the dried aromatic inner bark of certain tropical Asian trees that is used as a spice
conjured: to call or bring to mind

 ISBN-978-81-8477-738-3

Reading Comprehension

A. Answer the following questions.

Level 1

1. What do you remember from the poem? Try to answer the following questions without referring to the poem. After completing the exercise if you need to check, go through the poem once more.
   - What are the two names of the cook described in the poem?
   - What type of muffins does the cook make?
   - What daily meals are mentioned in verse 2?
   - What savoury dishes are prepared?
   - List some of the dishes mentioned in the poem in the table below. On the right-hand column, give a brief detail about it.

Name of the dish	Description

Level 2

2. What does "knowing by then where I came from" refer to?
3. What kind of person is Martha? Give instances from the poem to support your answer.
4. What imagery conjures up the sense of taste in verse 3? Why is this important to the speaker?

 ISBN-978-81-8477-738-3

5. Why was the speaker "happy and close, so close, to tears"?

6. Which part of the poem did you like the best? Explain why, taking into account the imagery used as well as the meaning.

B. Read the following note on "free-verse poem" and answer the following questions.

Level 3

The poem, *Yogurt and Cinnamon Dessert with Rose Geraniums and Peach*, is a free-verse poem. It does not have a regular rhythm. For example, these two lines have a different rhythm (beat).

> A little eager, a little shy,
> I walked into her kitchen that first morning

Many free-verse poems do contain rhyme, but they are not regular, and so you may not recognise them at first.

Free verse poems also contain examples of repetition, alliteration and other sound effects. All these techniques help to accentuate the language and reinforce the meaning of the poem.

7. Where is the rhyme in the following lines?

> Crisp bacon wrapped around soft seedless dates,
> dips with cheese and herbs.
> Served course-by-course, light pastas,
> the right wine, voices reverential as we ate.

8. Can you find examples of repetition and alliteration in the four lines given above?

9. Compose a five-line poem on your favourite food, referring to the discussion on free verse above. Remember, it should appeal to the senses of taste and smell.

 ISBN-978-81-8477-738-3

Vocabulary

There are many words in the English language that are from other languages. These are called **loanwords**.

Here is a list of loanwords and the country of their origin. You may be surprised!

Loanword	Country and language of origin
poodle	Germany
smuggle	Germany/Holland
tea	Malay
bonsai	Japan
geranium	Greece
kiosk	Persian
graffiti	Italian
bazaar	Persian

 ISBN-978-81-8477-738-3

A. We eat various kinds of food, but do you know where these dishes originally come from? Write down the country or countries or region of origin next to the food listed in the table below.

Dish	Country / countries
jerk chicken	
pizza	
rogan josh	
yorkshire pudding	
wonton noodle	
pumpernickel	
green curry	
couscous	
baclava	
daal	
sushi	
burger	

 ISBN-978-81-8477-738-3

B. Choose the correct "food" word from the box to complete the similes and idioms in the following sentences.

soup	cucumber	cheese	peas	beetroot	sardines

1. We really would be in the __________________ if we were caught cheating in an exam.
2. The passengers on the train were packed together like __________________.
3. John and I have been friends since we were at school. We like the same food; we play the same sports; we choose similar clothes. We're like two __________________ in a pod.
4. When she realised what she had done, Joyce went as red as a __________________.
5. Everyone else was starting to panic, but Tim was as cool as a __________________.
6. They may be twins but they're as different as chalk and __________________.

C. In each of the following lists of foods, circle the one which is different in some way from the other three and say why it is different.

1.	lemon	orange	grapefruit	tomato
2.	lobster	prawn	salmon	oyster
3.	fish	mutton	chicken	lamb
4.	ketchup	cream	butter	cheese
5.	apple	plum	rhubarb	grape

 ISBN-978-81-8477-738-3

D. Answer the following questions.

1. Why would a vegetarian not eat mutton and kidney pie?
2. If you don't like fish, would you enjoy sushi?

3. Why would a person who cannot eat milk products not eat a pizza?
4. Would a person who didn't like seafood eat lobsters?

5. Would a vegetarian eat spaghetti bolognese?

 ISBN-978-81-8477-738-3

Grammar

You may remember that when we use the **imperative**, the second person "you" is dropped as shown in the following example.

Please close the door.

(We are really saying: **You** please close the door.)

The imperative sentence is commonly used in recipes, like the one given below.

Add flour. Mix in the coconut milk.

Sometimes, it is used to give a command or to show annoyance or irritation.

Sometimes the imperative sentence has an **!**, particularly in everyday speech. For example:

Be quick! Don't go now! Try harder!

A. Work out what might be happening in the passage below. Then find the imperatives and underline them.

"Tell him to go home and sort things out, first. Otherwise, we'll have to set off without him," muttered Karim.

"Why me?" replied Meena, stepping forward and frowning.

"He'll listen to you."

 ISBN-978-81-8477-738-3

"Rubbish!"

"Go on – he will. He always listens to you."

"Just because he's my brother it doesn't mean he'll listen to me anymore than he'll listen to you. Go and tell him yourself!"

B. Decide what might happen next and write your own paragraph, including some imperatives.

C. Decide which of the following sentences are imperative sentences and then punctuate them correctly.

1. Get moving You'll miss the train if you don't hurry up
2. Are there any tomatoes left I thought he said there were some in the fridge
3. No No No Don't mend the puncture like that
4. I counted twenty-four books yesterday, but now there are only twenty-two
5. Get out of here Can't you see there are too many people in this lift already

 ISBN-978-81-8477-738-3

6. You're lucky to have such nourishing food. So eat it up
7. Does he always bring his dog with him
8. Did you tell your cousins about the holiday plans

D. The imperative sentence can be used as an impolite way of expressing ourselves. Rewrite the following imperative sentences in a polite way.

1. Stop it now!
2. Leave your brother alone!
3. Get out of my way!
4. Don't forget the key again!
5. Never do that again!

Listening

Listen to the text and answer the questions given below.

1. What was a farmer's main role in the early phase / stage of agriculture?
2. What would the farmer's year be governed by?
3. What was a market for?
4. What does "barter" mean?
5. Who might take a portion of the farmer's income?
6. In what way has the consumption of food changed?

 ISBN-978-81-8477-738-3

7. What might the speaker mean by food that is "highly processed"? Write down some processed food.

Processed food
1.
2.
3.
4.
5.
6.

Speaking

A. Read the following poem by Fred Sedgwick.

Mr Khan's Shop
is dark and beautiful.
There are parathas,

garam masala,
naan breads full of fruit.

There are bhajis, samosas, dhal,
garlic, ground cumin seeds.

shiny emerald chillies
lie like incendiary bombs.

 ISBN-978-81-8477-738-3

There are bhindi in sacks,
aloo to eat with hot puris

and mango pickle. There's
rice, yoghurt,

cucumber and mint–
raita to cool the tongue.

Sometimes you see
Where the shop darkens.

Mr Khan, his wife
and their children

round the table.
The smells have come alive.

He serves me
poppadoms, smiles,

re-enters the dark.
Perhaps one day

He'll ask me to dine with them:
bhajis, samosas, pakoras,

 ISBN-978-81-8477-738-3

coriander, dhal.
I'll give him this poem: *Sit down*

young man, he'll say,
and eat your words.

1. Now work with a partner to make a presentation for a large group (about eight) for which you need to decide on the following points.
   - Who will read what lines
   - How you will stand
   - Who will introduce the poem
   - How the poem will be introduced
2. If you have time, memorise the poem.

 ISBN-978-81-8477-738-3

Writing

Write a free-verse poem of your own, choosing as your topic something particularly delicious, such as a dessert or your favourite food.

1. You will need to make it sound appealing.
2. While composing your poem, keep the following points in mind.
   - When you write a free-verse poem, you do not have a regular rhythm.
   - Many free-verse poems do have rhymes, but they are not usually obvious.
3. Give an interesting title to your poem.

Activity

Write a detailed recipe for a dessert.

1. You can select the ingredients from any part of the world, but the recipe should be your own and remember to include the following points.
   - the number of people the recipe is for
   - a list of ingredients
   - the preparation process
   - cooking time (if required to be mentioned)
   - presentation
2. You should try to write the recipe correctly, using the appropriate style. You can also look at a series of recipes from different cookery books to study the layout. However, the recipe should be your own invention.

Remember

The imperative is often used in recipes.

 ISBN-978-81-8477-738-3

2 Chocolates

When he was thirteen years old, Roald Dahl was sent to the Repton Public School for boys. It was a boarding school where the boys belonged to different "Houses" within the school. The following excerpt from the book *Boy: Tales of Childhood* by Dahl describes one of his experiences there.

1 Every now and again, a plain grey cardboard box was dished out to each boy in our House, and this, believe it or not, was a present from the great chocolate manufacturers, Cadbury. Inside the box there were twelve bars of chocolate, all of different shapes, all with different fillings and all with numbers from one to twelve stamped on the chocolate **underneath**. Eleven of these bars were new inventions from the factory. The twelfth was the "control" bar, one that we all knew well, usually a Cadbury's Coffee Cream bar. Also in the box was a sheet of paper with the numbers one to twelve on it as well as two blank columns, one for giving marks to each chocolate from **nought** to ten, and the other for comments.

2 And all we were required to do in return for this splendid gift was to taste very carefully each bar of chocolate, give it marks and make an intelligent comment on why we liked it or disliked it.

Were the boys happy to receive the chocolate bars? How do you know?

3 It was a clever stunt. Cadbury's were using some of the greatest chocolate-bar experts in the world to test out their new inventions. We were of a sensible age, between thirteen and eighteen, and we knew intimately every chocolate bar in existence, from the Milk Flake to the Lemon Marshmallow. Quite obviously our opinions on anything new would be valuable. All of us entered into this game with great gusto,

---

underneath: in or to a place beneath, below
nought: variant of naught, meaning nothingness

 ISBN-978-81-8477-738-3

sitting in our studies and nibbling each bar with the air of connoisseurs, giving our marks and making our comments. "Too subtle for the common palate," was one note that I remember writing down.

4 For me, the importance of all this was that I began to realise that the large chocolate companies actually did possess inventing rooms and they took their inventing very seriously. I used to picture a long white room like a laboratory with pots of chocolate and fudge and all sorts of other delicious fillings bubbling away on the stoves, while men and women in white coats moved between the bubbling pots, tasting and mixing and **concocting** their wonderful new inventions. I used to imagine myself working in one of these labs and suddenly I would come up with something so absolutely unbearably delicious that I would grab it in my hand and go rushing out of the lab and along the corridor and right into the office of the great Mr Cadbury himself. "I've got it, sir!" I would shout, putting the chocolate in front of him. "It's fantastic! It's fabulous! It's marvellous! It's irresistible!"

What images are created in this paragraph?

concocting: to prepare by mixing ingredients, as in cooking; to devise, using skill and intelligence

 ISBN-978-81-8477-738-3

5 Slowly the great man would pick up my newly invented chocolate and he would take a small bite. He would roll it round his mouth. Then all at once, he would leap up from his chair, crying, "You've got it! You've done it! It's a miracle!" He would slap me on the back and shout, "We'll sell it by the million! We'll sweep the world with this one! How on earth did you do it? Your salary is doubled!"

6 It was lovely dreaming those dreams, and I have no doubt at all that, thirty-five years later, when I was looking for a plot for my second book for children, I remembered those little cardboard boxes and the newly-invented chocolates inside them, and I began to write a book called *Charlie and the Chocolate Factory*.

Reading Comprehension

A. Answer the following questions.

Level 1

1. What do you remember from the passage? Try to answer the following questions without referring to the excerpt. After completing the exercise if you need to check, go through the passage once more.
    - Which company used to send the chocolates?
    - How many bars of chocolate were there and how were they organised?
    - How many of them were new recipes?
    - What kind of chocolate was the "control bar"?
    - Which book by Roald Dahl came out of the chocolate-testing experience?

Level 2

2. What was the purpose of the "control bar"?
3. Who are the "greatest chocolate-bar experts"? Do you agree? Why or why not?

4. What does the description "too subtle for the common palate" mean?

5. Find three descriptions used by the author in paragraph 4 that appeal to the sense of taste.

6. What do you think was the most interesting part of the excerpt? Why?

B. Study the SPSE pattern.

Level 3

Sometimes we can apply an organisational pattern – SPSE or **S**ituation **P**roblem **S**olution **E**valuation – to a text concerned with problems and solutions.

Situation →	Problem →	Solution →	Evaluation
The general circumstances	The specific difficulty	The answer: there might be more than one answer, or it might be changed or added to	Whether or not the specific problem has been solved or seems to have been solved

7. Do you think SPSE works in the excerpt, *Chocolates*? In what way does Roald Dahl introduce comedy into the formula? Discuss with a friend and decide between yourselves. Do make notes.

Situation	Problem	Solution	Evaluation

8. In the excerpt, the phrase "a clever stunt" is used in paragraph 3. What does it refer to and how does it relate to question 7.

 ISBN-978-81-8477-738-3

Vocabulary

There are many useful words that are specifically used to describe a problem or a solution.

For example:
To describe a problem → complex, complication, tricky, trouble, mess, crunch
To describe a solution → result, key, resolution, answer, solving.

A. Circle the words given below that are used to describe problems and solutions.

like	difficulty	consequently	objection	opposing	doubt
meanwhile	dilemma	predicament	such as	obstacle	after
unresolved	puzzle	answer	next	resolving	unlike
sorting out	too	severe	satisfy	agree	otherwise
also	suited	appropriate	opportunity	adapt	therefore

B. The words that are not circled in question A are connectors. Put these words in the table below and identify the type of connector for each one. The first one has been done for you.

Connector	Type
like	comparison

 ISBN-978-81-8477-738-3

C. Write synonyms for the following words from the passage.

1. gusto
2. intimately
3. expertise
4. connoisseur
5. palate
6. irresistible
7. concocting

D. Identify the words indicating of problem or solution in these sentences. There may be more than one in each sentence.

1. He was very concerned about the infection, which seemed to be spreading.
2. The timetable was the perfect answer to all their difficulties.
3. It was a predicament since she had promised to go to the museum with her mother and the art gallery with her cousin on the same day.
4. It was a puzzle that she was determined to solve by the end of the lesson.

 ISBN-978-81-8477-738-3

Grammar

We use the **past continuous tense** to refer to actions that were ongoing at a certain point in the past. See the following examples.

Cadbury's **were using** some of the greatest chocolate-bar experts in the world to test out their new inventions.

I **was looking** for a plot for my second book.

We use the **future tense** when talking about future actions as shown in the example below.

I **will create** a new recipe for their anniversary.

We use the **future continuous tense** when talking about things that will be ongoing at a certain point in the future. See the following example.

I **will be creating** a new recipe for their anniversary.

A. Complete the sentences below using your own ideas.

1. So many delicious smells were wafting...
2. Inside the lab he was inventing...
3. They were creating...
4. We were having...
5. Nobody was walking...

 ISBN-978-81-8477-738-3

B. Change the following sentences from past continuous tense to past tense.

1. He was playing his drums so loudly his parents couldn't hear themselves speak.
2. Scruff and Rover were chasing each other round and round the pond.
3. Jack and Minnie were skating around the ice rink while everyone clapped.

C. Change the following sentences from the future tense to the future continuous tense.

1. He won't see her before lunch.
2. I'll leave in twenty minutes for the restaurant.
3. Will they see her at the cookery competition?
4. The new café will open on 1 July.
5. Maybe we'll go out for dinner.

D. Change the following sentences from the future continuous tense to future tense.

1. They will be waiting for you at the cinema so make sure you get there on time.
2. They shall be expecting the letter to arrive tomorrow by the morning post.
3. We'll be staying at the hotel for three nights and then we'll be getting the train to Zurich.

 ISBN-978-81-8477-738-3

E. Fill in the blanks in the following sentences with verbs in the past continuous tense, using the words provided in the box.

watch	play	rain	look

1. I ______________ television when the phone rang.
2. It ______________ heavily by the time we reached the hotel.
3. The boys ______________ cricket in the street when one of them hit the ball through a window.
4. The boy ______________ anxiously out of the window.

F. Write a paragraph using the past continuous tense to describe a new chocolate recipe that is being created. You may use the sentences from question A in your paragraph.

Listening

Listen to the text and answer the following questions.

1. What does "economic miracle" refer to?
2. Why have cars increased?
3. There are five main problems mentioned. What are they?
4. In what instance might a car not be useful?
5. Who are most likely to be affected by pollution?

 ISBN-978-81-8477-738-3

Speaking

Following on from "Listening," consider some solutions to lessen the problems of traffic in cities.

1. Make notes on the possible solutions.
2. Memorise your points. List them in the table below.

Problem	Solution

3. Prepare a talk on traffic problems and their solutions to be given to a large group (about eight students).
4. Introduce your talk and present it to the group.

Writing

Find out how cities in other countries deal with their traffic problems.

1. Make notes. If you are going to use the Internet, check with your teacher first.
2. Using your notes and the work you have done in "Listening" and "Speaking," write a problem / solution account called "City Traffic: Problems and Solutions".

 ISBN-978-81-8477-738-3

Activity

A. Collect some data and facts on traffic in the following cities.

1. Mumbai
2. London
3. Beijing

B. You can decide on the kind of facts, information and data to be included. (For example, the number of vehicles travelling through the city over a given period, speed limits, traffic offences, road accidents, traffic improvements.)

C. Choose a way of presenting your data. Some suggestions are listed below.

1. a fact file
2. a table
3. a timeline (if you are presenting information over a period of time)
4. a combination of presentations

 ISBN-978-81-8477-738-3

The Environment

Study the pictures and discuss the following questions with a partner.

1. Describe what is happening in the pictures. What do they suggest about polar bears?
2. Do you know what conditions polar bears need to thrive in?

 ISBN-978-81-8477-738-3

3 The Future of the Polar Bear

Read the following account by Mary Green.

1 The lion, the tiger, the elephant and the polar bear – everyone has heard of them, even little children, and we assume these animals will always be with us. Yet each one is an **endangered** species. The Bali tiger has already become **extinct**. Other species of tiger along with the Indian elephant are at high risk, and the lion, African elephant and polar bear are vulnerable.

2 There are many reasons for this state of affairs. Land development, whether through farming, industry or the growth of communities, alters or destroys an animal's natural habitat, as does climate change. Poaching for animal parts can dramatically reduce the number of species (such as tusk ivory in the case of the elephant). Any exploitation of the earth's natural resources has its effect.

3 The polar bear is being directly affected by climate change. The Arctic Circle and the surrounding land and seas are its habitat. To understand why it is threatened we need to know how it has adapted. It is a close relative of the brown bear, but it has adjusted to live in extreme conditions. It can accommodate freezing temperatures, move across ice and snow and swim in Arctic water. Its main source of food is the seal, which it hunts from ice floes.

4 Sea ice is crucial to its survival, which it travels across to reach its prey and also to breed. The ice sheets are shrinking. Since 1950, the summer thickness of the ice has decreased radically and it is thought that by 2050 there may be no summer ice. Polar bears can swim for many miles, but as the ice decreases the distances become too great. If the bear

---

endangered: seriously at the risk of extinction
extinct: no longer in existence

 ISBN-978-81-8477-738-3

cannot hunt sufficiently, it cannot build up fat reserves to see it through the winter; hence, it starves. The bear also depends on snow caves, called maternity dens, to rear its young. These occur in thick snowdrifts and provide protection and warmth. However, rising temperatures mean that the dens can collapse. Dens are also threatened by the oil industry. Apart from the dangers of pollution, the search for oil can disrupt the bears' breeding grounds. This might result in female bears leaving their dens early, which may lead to the death of the young ones.

5 The indigenous people of the Arctic are threatened by climate change too. Their culture has evolved to deal with extreme conditions. Like the polar bear, they hunt the seal and are affected by thinning ice. The bear is also part of their culture and history. There are many folk tales and spiritual beliefs that reveal how closely their lives are entwined and the polar bear's decline is also a warning for those who care about the survival of the **indigenous** people of the Arctic region.

6 Can the polar bear survive? No one knows. Some believe they might adapt to become a land species hunting for different food, but if so, would there be sufficient food available? The polar bear would be competing with other animals, including other bears. And if they did adapt, they might also mate with other bear species, such as the brown bear. In which case would they still be polar bears?

---

indigenous: native, originating or occurring naturally in a particular place

 ISBN-978-81-8477-738-3

Reading Comprehension

Answer the following questions.

Level 1

1. Which type of tiger is already extinct? Which type of elephant is at high risk of extinction?
2. Which animals apart from the polar bear are "vulnerable"?
3. Name two ways through which the land can be developed to save endangered animals.
4. Where can the polar bear be found?
5. What is the polar bear's main food?
6. What are snow caves used for?

Level 2

7. Do you think that the public would be shocked to hear how many animals are on the endangered list? Why or why not?
8. What is the main difference between the polar bear and the brown bear?
9. What do you think is the attitude of indigenous people towards the polar bear?
10. What do you think is the most important reason for the threat to the polar bear?
11. In what sense might polar bears survive, but will no longer remain as polar bears?

Level 3

12. Work with a partner to draw up a conservation plan that you think would help the polar bear.
    - Try to think of three key points. Note them down in the following table.

 ISBN-978-81-8477-738-3

Problem and Possible Solution	

- Working on your own, write up the key points as a paragraph. Then check it with your partner and redraft it as needed.

Vocabulary

A. Provide synonyms and antonyms for the words. They are taken from the passage. Try not to refer to a thesaurus.

Word	Synonym	Antonym
endangered		
extinct		
vulnerable		
exploitation		
crucial		
maternity		
indigenous		

 ISBN-978-81-8477-738-3

B. Circle the word that is not a synonym of the word in bold print.

1.	**outcome**	consequence	desire	effect	result
2.	**change**	modify	alter	invent	transform
3.	**protect**	defend	destroy	guard	preserve
4.	**maintain**	argue	state	confuse	believe
5.	**wise**	sensible	imaginary	prudent	judicious

C. Using *un-*, *in-* or *dis-*, form the antonyms of the following words.

For example:
happy → unhappy

1. important
2. complete
3. agreement
4. enthusiastic
5. sufficient
6. common
7. satisfactory
8. satisfied
9. similar
10. natural
11. frequent
12. accurate

 ISBN-978-81-8477-738-3

D. Use the prefixes provided below to form antonyms of the following words.

dis- il- im- in- ir- mis- un-

1. mask
2. mobile
3. fortune
4. bar
5. relevant
6. legible
7. fertile
8. mortal
9. regular
10. associate
11. acceptable
12. lead
13. reversible
14. concerned

 ISBN-978-81-8477-738-3

Grammar

Colon (**:**) is a punctuation mark that is used in a dialogue to show the words spoken by someone. **Quotation marks** (**"..."**) are not needed in a dialogue.
See the following example.

Joe**:** Why is sea ice crucial for polar bears?
Jane**:** It is needed for hunting and breeding.

In order to make a conversation sound natural, you may need to include **question marks** (**?**) and **exclamation marks** (**!**) wherever appropriate.

A. Read the following information about the Bali tiger.

The Bali tiger was last seen in the 1930s, although it may have survived beyond that. Today, there are none left. It was a subspecies of the tiger, similar in size to a leopard and only found on Bali, a small Indonesian island. It became extinct largely due to hunting and the destruction of its habitat. Several other subspecies, such as the Javan tiger, have also become extinct.

Use the information about Bali tigers to complete this conversation between two characters. Follow the guidelines below.

Jamal: Did you know that the Bali tiger was extinct?

- Give a name to the second character who will participate in this conversation.
- Try to make the conversation sound natural.
- Try to imagine a scene for your characters. For example, is Jamal reading a book? Has he seen a television programme? How does he know about the Bali tiger?
- Check that your punctuation is correct. Use question marks and exclamation marks, where necessary.

 ISBN-978-81-8477-738-3

B. The following note was left on the fridge door. Write it out correctly using colons and commas and any other punctuation you think is necessary.

ben

please buy the following from the hardware store white paint paintbrushes cloths paint roller and tray and also a scraper Oh and please don't forget a hammer

can you also ask joy to collect these items from the cleaners dad's suit my green dress and the blue curtains

hope you can manage all this between you

thanks

mum

Listening

Listen to the text and answer the following questions.

1. In what ways have humans profoundly changed the natural environment?
2. Why do rainforest tribes move on after a few years?
3. Why is it important for tribes to move on and settle elsewhere?
4. Name an example of a large-scale enterprise that destroys the rainforest.
5. What effect does the destruction of the rainforest have?

 ISBN-978-81-8477-738-3

Speaking

Work in small groups (no more than four) to discuss the following questions.

1. In what way do humans always affect the environment and wildlife? Write your notes in the boxes.

Animal	Human action	Effect

2. How can we successfully cohabit with wildlife?

   Appoint a recorder to note the points and a reporter to report your discussion to another group.

Writing

Write an account about animals that are at risk of extinction.

 ISBN-978-81-8477-738-3

1. You will need to carry out some investigations. The International Union for Conservation of Nature (IUCN) has a Red List that gives information about whether or not a species is threatened. Some categories are listed below.

Near Threatened (NT)	may be threatened soon
Vulnerable (VU)	high risk of extinction in the future
Endangered (EN)	very high risk of extinction in the future
Critically Endangered (CR)	extremely high risk of extinction in the near future
Extinct in the Wild (EW)	no species left in the wild, but some species in captivity
Extinct (E)	no species left

2. Choose a few animals that appear in different categories and write a paragraph about each. Include the following points.
    - Where it lives and what its habitat is like
    - Why it is endangered
    - What, if anything, is being done to curb its decline
3. Include an introduction and conclusion for the write-up.

Activity

The polar bear appears as a figure or motif in many cultures. It appears on logos, stamps, in literature and legend. Carry out an investigation on the different depictions of the polar bear.

1. Explain the following.
    - Where the examples come from
    - What they mean (for instance, in a story or as a symbol of a conservation group)

 ISBN-978-81-8477-738-3

Depiction	Country	Meaning/stands for

2. Organise the information to make it reader-friendly. Apart from the written text, include or choose from the following features.
   - diagrams
   - illustrations
   - fact files
   - timelines
3. Think about how you will present your material. Will it be on a screen, as a poster or a leaflet, or will you use more than one kind of presentation?

 ISBN-978-81-8477-738-3

4 Climate Change and Renewable Energy

An **investigative text** is similar to a text involving a problem and a solution, but it does not necessarily provide a solution. It investigates the topic and explores possibilities. Many information texts will contain investigative texts within them, particularly if they are concerned with topics where there are no simple answers, such as climate change. An investigative text will:

- present the issue
- explore possibilities by making a series of logical points or ideas
- draw conclusions, sometimes expressing an opinion.

The following is an example of an investigative text. It is an excerpt from *Climate Change* by John Woodward (2008). Read it.

Green Transport

presents the issue

The transport of people and freight accounts for at least 14 per cent of global greenhouse gas emissions. This figure is increasing, especially in many developing nations. **Technology may help through the development of more efficient vehicles, powered by less polluting fuels. But most of the more exciting proposals are still in the design stage, and some may not work in practice.**

makes two logical points

 ISBN-978-81-8477-738-3

So in the short term, the best way to reduce greenhouse gas emissions from transport is to change the way we travel and not travel so much.

draws conclusions by expressing an opinion

A. Skim the text below using the headings, sub-headings and topic sentences (usually the first sentence in each paragraph) to get a general idea of what the text is about.

B. Read the text again and find the following.

- the issue being presented
- the main point being made
- the conclusion being drawn

C. Make short notes about what the text is about in general. Do not list every point being made. Search for what the points have in common and the conclusion drawn.

Remember

- When you skim a text, you are trying to gain the overall meaning.
- When you scan a text, you are searching for specific information.

Renewable energy

1 For centuries people have been harnessing the energy of wind and flowing water to power windmills and watermills. This technology has now been updated to drive electricity generators. Solar energy and even volcanic heat can also be turned into electricity. Such energy sources are described as renewable because they never run out. They may not be able to provide all our energy needs, but most of them do not release any of the greenhouse gases that are causing climate change.

 ISBN-978-81-8477-738-3

Wind Farms

2 Wind is already being **harnessed** on a large scale by "wind farms" of hi-tech wind turbines. Many are sited on land, often in hilly, scenic regions where people resent their impact on the landscape. Offshore wind farms, such as this one near Copenhagen, Denmark, experience stronger, more consistent winds and they can be built well away from land, although there are concerns about seabirds being killed by the huge rotors. The main practical problem is that wind turbines work only when the wind blows. This means that there must be back-up power generator systems, which often have to use fossil fuels.

Solar power plants

3 Most solar power systems are small-scale, but a few big power plants have been built in reliably sunny regions such as California and Spain. They use mirrors to focus the sun's rays on a tower that collects the heat and uses it to run a turbine and generator. More efficient power lines may enable such plants to distribute power to cities in less sunny areas.

Hydro-electric power

4 Rainwater flowing off the land can be used to power turbines linked to electricity generators. To ensure a steady flow the water is stored in reservoirs created by building huge dams across upland river valleys. This means that the power plants can be built only in suitable terrain. The dams can cause serious problems for wildlife, and the reservoirs often silt up. But hydro-electric power is a proven, dependable technology that currently supplies 15 per cent of the world's electricity.

---

harnessed: control and make use of (natural resources), especially to produce energy

 ISBN-978-81-8477-738-3

Energy efficiency

5 Supplying power without using the fossil fuels that contribute to climate change is not easy. Wind farms, for example, produce far less electricity than fuel-burning power plants, and the wind does not blow all the time. But if we all used less energy, technologies such as wind and solar power would be able to cope with a bigger proportion of the demand. We can help to improve this by improving energy efficiency, or making sure things use less power to do the same job. This applies both to the people who design equipment, and to the people who use it.

Reading Comprehension

A. Answer the following questions.

Level 1

1. Scan the text to find out specific answers to the questions below. Time yourself!
    - What has energy from the wind and flowing water been used for in the past?
    - What are the more recent uses of wind and flowing water?
    - Apart from solar energy what else, mentioned in the text, produces heat in the natural world?
    - What does renewable energy mean?

 ISBN-978-81-8477-738-3

- What causes climate change?
- What is the main problem with windmills?

Level 2

2. Are you in favour of wind farms? Why or why not? Think about the advantages and disadvantages.
3. What is solar energy? Are you in favour of solar energy in India? Why or why not? (Remember to take the climate into consideration.)
4. What do you think we should all do to help use less energy?

Level 3

B. Read the following and answer the questions.

Climate change and the increase in global temperatures – these two issues concern people and governments alike. No one knows exactly what will happen, but scientists and environmentalists are exploring ways of reducing the effects of a changing climate on our planet and the many species, including ourselves, that live on it. An important task for us is to reduce greenhouse gas emissions – the gases that are warming the planet. These are largely caused by the burning of fossil fuels, such as oil and coal, and by our modern lifestyles.

5. Explain the following.
   - the issue being presented
   - the main point being made
   - the conclusion being drawn
6. Using prior knowledge, give two examples of how our modern lifestyle contributes to global warming.

 ISBN-978-81-8477-738-3

Vocabulary

A. Write down the definition of the following technical terms. Use a dictionary if you need to.

1. generator

2. renewable energy

3. energy efficiency

4. offshore wind farms

5. turbine

6. reservoir

7. hydro-electric power

8. fossil fuels

B. Write down the definition of these words without using a dictionary. Then check your answers.

1. environment

2. conservation

3. locality

 ISBN-978-81-8477-738-3

4. global

5. agriculture

6. sustainable

7. deforestation

Grammar

Modal verbs are commonly found in investigative texts because they allow us to explore possibilities. They are words like "would", "can", "could", "should", "may", "might", "ought", "must". For example:

We **should** be aware of how much energy we use. Then we **may** find that we **can** easily cut down our energy consumption.

We can use several verbs as **semi-modal verbs** such as the verbs "used" and "ought". They are both used with a "to" infinitive, so it is best to think of them as "ought to" and "used to".

"used to" is a past tense verb and it refers to things in the past.

I **used to** go to the cinema once a week.

"ought to" functions in the same way as "should".

I **ought to** buy tickets for the festival today.

I **should** buy tickets for the festival today.

 ISBN-978-81-8477-738-3

A. Work with a partner.

1. Write down what you think a modal verb can do.
2. Discuss why the above text uses modal verbs.

B. Working alone, find four different examples of modal verbs in the main text on pages 48–50.

C. Write a paragraph using the writing frame below. Include modal verbs in the write-up.

In the future, climate change...

In addition, there...

and we...

Finally...

D. Using the modal verbs and main verbs given in square brackets, rewrite this dialogue converting the modal verbs into the past tense.

For example:
"(could; go)" → "could have gone".

Mother: You know, you really ought to clean your shoes more often, Simon.

Simon: Yes, I know. I (ought; clean) them this morning. I (would; shine) them before I went out, but I didn't leave myself enough time.
I (should; get up) earlier. I (could; do) them last night, but I forgot.
I (must; have) something else on my mind. If I had thought about it, I (might; polish) them yesterday afternoon, but it didn't occur to me. I'll go and clean them now.

 ISBN-978-81-8477-738-3

E. Pick out the modal verbs in the following sentences.

1. Many people wonder how they can help to reduce the emission of greenhouse gases into the atmosphere.
2. We must do more to combat climate change.
3. Temperatures might rise by as much as 5 degrees.
4. The cost would be considerable, but it could save you a lot of money in the end.
5. We must act now, not in 10 years' time when it may be too late.
6. People ought to be more careful about what they throw away.
7. One might say that we should avoid the use of batteries as much as we can.
8. Can we afford to wait until we know all the facts?
9. Would you like to have a wind turbine on the roof of your house?
10. We should not assume that technology can solve all the problems that might arise.

F. Finish the following sentences using either "used to" or "ought to". Remember to punctuate the sentences correctly.

1. Last year...
2. I'm late this morning, so...
3. Long ago when the world was new...
4. Can you remember when we were small we always...
5. When the vegetables are chopped...
6. If the computer screen goes blank again...
7. In the past people...
8. Regarding your new bike, you...

 ISBN-978-81-8477-738-3

G. Look back over the sentences you have just written. Are there any other modal verbs being used? Underline them.

Listening

Listen to the text about nuclear energy and answer the following questions.

1. In what way is nuclear energy non-polluting?
2. Where does nuclear energy come from?
3. What is the problem with uranium?
4. What else can a reactor be used for?

 ISBN-978-81-8477-738-3

Speaking

Work in a group of four to discuss whether or not nuclear energy should be used as an alternative source of energy.

1. Recollect the work you have already done and your general knowledge about renewable energy from wind farms and solar energy.
2. Follow the instructions collectively.
   - Draw up a "for and against" table and record points.
   - Appoint one person to act as the recorder.
   - Appoint another person to report back to the class.
   - Come to an agreement within the group before reporting back.
3. You may need to carry out further research on nuclear energy. If you use the Internet, you should do so with your teacher's guidance.

Writing

Drawing on the work you have done in this unit, write an account about climate change and renewable energy. Use your own words and ideas. Write about 500 words.

1. Include the following in your write-up.
   - Information on climate change: this may include your own knowledge and further investigation (for example, about the greenhouse effect, the long-term possible effects of global warming, etc.).
   - What renewable energy is and why we need it: you should also mention other types of renewable energy as well as those mentioned here.

 ISBN-978-81-8477-738-3

2. Remember to include the following points from the passage.
   - the issues being presented (there will be more than one)
   - the main points being made
   - the conclusions being drawn

Activity

A. Find out how climate change is affecting or being affected by one of the following.

- The Maldives
- The Amazon Rain Forest
- The Great Barrier Reef in Australia

B. Write short notes in the box and present your findings as a talk.

Notes

1. Try not to read your work from paper or a screen. Become sufficiently familiar with it so that you do not need your notes.
2. Refer to evidence to support your points. You could, for example, use tables, graphs or photos.

 ISBN-978-81-8477-738-3

Theme 3

Cautionary Tales

Study the picture and discuss the following questions with a partner.

1. What is the time or era in which the picture is set?
2. How would you describe the scene in the picture?
3. What details do you notice in particular and why?
4. How can you tell that it depicts a fantasy?

 ISBN-978-81-8477-738-3

5 The Lady of Shalott

Read the following poem by Alfred Lord Tennyson.

Part I

1 On either side the river lie
Long fields of barley and of rye,
That clothe the **wold** and meet the sky;
And thro' the field the road runs by
    To many-tower'd Camelot;
And up and down the people go,
Gazing where the lilies blow
Round an island there below,
    The island of Shalott.

2 Willows whiten, **aspens** quiver,
Little breezes dusk and shiver
Thro' the wave that runs for ever
By the island in the river
    Flowing down to Camelot.
Four gray walls, and four gray towers,
Overlook a space of flowers,
And the silent isle **imbowers**
    The Lady of Shalott.

3 By the margin, willow veil'd,
Slide the heavy barges trail'd
By slow horses; and unhail'd
The **shallop** flitteth silken-sail'd
    Skimming down to Camelot:

---

wold: upland
aspens: type of poplar
imbowers: surrounds
shallop: shallow water boat

 ISBN-978-81-8477-738-3

But who hath seen her wave her hand?
Or at the **casement** seen her stand?
Or is she known in all the land,
    The Lady of Shalott?

4 Only reapers, reaping early
In among the bearded barley,
Hear a song that echoes cheerly
From the river winding clearly,

    Down to tower'd Camelot:
And by the moon the reaper weary,
Piling **sheaves** in uplands airy,
Listening, whispers " 'Tis the fairy
    Lady of Shalott."

Part II

5 There she weaves by night and day
A magic web with colours gay.
She has heard a whisper say,
A curse is on her if she stay
    To look down to Camelot.
She knows not what the curse may be,
And so she weaveth steadily,
And little other care hath she,
    The Lady of Shalott.

6 And moving thro' a mirror clear
That hangs before her all the year,
Shadows of the world appear.
There she sees the highway near
    Winding down to Camelot:
There the river eddy whirls,

---

casement: hinged window
sheaves: bundles of wheat stalks

 ISBN-978-81-8477-738-3

And there the surly **village-churls**,
And the red cloaks of market girls,
    Pass onward from Shalott.

7 Sometimes a troop of damsels glad,
An abbot on an **ambling pad**,
Sometimes a curly shepherd-lad,
Or long-hair'd page in crimson clad,
    Goes by to tower'd Camelot;
And sometimes thro' the mirror blue
The knights come riding two and two:
She hath no loyal knight and true,
    The Lady of Shalott.

8 But in her web she still delights
To weave the mirror's magic sights,
For often thro' the silent nights
A funeral, with plumes and lights
    And music, went to Camelot:
Or when the moon was overhead,
Came two young lovers lately wed;
"I am half sick of shadows," said
    The Lady of Shalott.

Part III

9 A bow-shot from her bower-eaves,
He rode between the barley-sheaves,
The sun came dazzling thro' the leaves,
And flamed upon the brazen greaves
    Of bold Sir Lancelot.
A red-cross knight for ever kneel'd
To a lady in his shield,
That sparkled on the yellow field,
    Beside remote Shalott.

---

village-churls: rough-mannered villagers
ambling pad: saddle

 ISBN-978-81-8477-738-3

10 The gemmy **bridle glitter'd** free,
Like to some branch of stars we see
Hung in the golden Galaxy.
The bridle bells rang merrily
    As he rode down to Camelot:
And from his blazon'd **baldric** slung
A mighty silver bugle hung,
And as he rode his armour rung,
    Beside remote Shalott.

11 All in the blue unclouded weather
Thick-jewell'd shone the saddle-leather,
The helmet and the helmet-feather
Burn'd like one burning flame together,
    As he rode down to Camelot.
As often thro' the purple night,
Below the starry clusters bright,
Some bearded meteor, trailing light,
    Moves over still Shalott.

12 His broad clear brow in sunlight glow'd;
On burnish'd hooves his war-horse trode;
From underneath his helmet flow'd
His coal-black curls as on he rode,
    As he rode down to Camelot.
From the bank and from the river
He flash'd into the crystal mirror,
"Tirra lirra," by the river
    Sang Sir Lancelot.

13 She left the web, she left the loom,
She made three paces thro' the room,
She saw the water-lily bloom,

---

bridle glitter'd: glittering harness
baldric: leather belt

 ISBN-978-81-8477-738-3

She saw the helmet and the plume,
    She look'd down to Camelot.
Out flew the web and floated wide;
The mirror crack'd from side to side;
"The curse is come upon me," cried
    The Lady of Shalott.

Part IV

14 In the stormy east-wind straining,
The pale yellow woods were waning,
The broad stream in his banks complaining,
Heavily the low sky raining
    Over tower'd Camelot;
Down she came and found a boat
Beneath a willow left afloat,
And round about the prow she wrote
    The Lady of Shalott.

15 And down the river's dim expanse
Like some bold seër in a trance,
Seeing all his own mischance–
With a glassy countenance
    Did she look to Camelot.
And at the closing of the day
She loosed the chain, and down she lay;
The broad stream bore her far away,
    The Lady of Shalott.

16 Lying, robed in snowy white
That loosely flew to left and right–
The leaves upon her falling light–
Thro' the noises of the night
    She floated down to Camelot:
And as the boat-head wound along
The willowy hills and fields among,
They heard her singing her last song,
    The Lady of Shalott.

 ISBN-978-81-8477-738-3

17 Heard a carol, mournful, holy,
Chanted loudly, chanted lowly,
Till her blood was frozen slowly,
And her eyes were darken'd wholly,
Turn'd to tower'd Camelot.
For ere she reach'd upon the tide
The first house by the water-side,
Singing in her song she died,
The Lady of Shalott.

18 Under tower and balcony,
By garden-wall and gallery,
A gleaming shape she floated by,
Dead-pale between the houses high,
Silent into Camelot.
Out upon the wharfs they came,
Knight and burgher, lord and dame,
And round the prow they read her name,
The Lady of Shalott.

19 Who is this? And what is here?
And in the lighted palace near
Died the sound of royal cheer;
And they cross'd themselves for fear,
All the knights at Camelot:
But Lancelot mused a little space;
He said, "She has a lovely face;
God in his mercy lend her grace,
The Lady of Shalott."

 ISBN-978-81-8477-738-3

Reading Comprehension

A. Answer the following questions.

Level 1

1. Scan parts I and II of the poem to find out information.
   - Where does the Lady of Shalott live?
   - What line in the first verse describes Camelot?
   - Mention three things one notices in the journey down to the Camelot in verse 3 of Part I?
   - When could the curse on the Lady of Shalott take effect?
   - What (in general) moves through the mirror that hangs in front of the Lady of Shalott?

Level 2

2. Who do you think the Lady of Shalott is? Look for evidence in the text to support your comments.
3. How does Sir Lancelot affect the Lady of Shalott?
4. How does the curse affect the Lady of Shalott?

B. Read the following note on metre in poetry and answer the questions.

Metre is the pattern of rhythm in verse and is referred to when discussing regular repeating patterns in poetry. It is the pattern of stressed and unstressed syllables.

/ = stressed

u = unstressed

 ISBN-978-81-8477-738-3

For example:

On either side the river lie

u / u / u /u /

This pattern of stressed and unstressed syllables is called **iambic**.

The line above has four feet (units) that are unstressed and stressed. We call this tetrameter. So the metre of the line is **iambic tetrameter.**

There are other patterns of stressed and unstressed syllables and a variety of feet. Look at the information in the box below.

Common Metres

u / iamb (iambic) **uu/** anapaest (anapaestic) **/u** trochee (trochaic)

/uu dactyl (dactylic) **//** spondee (spondaic) **uu** pyrrhic

1 foot = monometer 2 feet = dimeter 3 feet = trimeter

4 feet = tetrameter 5 feet = pentameter 6 feet = hexameter

Examples from poems

The following are additional examples of feet and metre combinations.

Iambic Pentameter

From *On His Blindness*, by John Milton

1 2 3 4 5

When **I** | con **SID** | er **HOW** | my **LIFE** | is **SPENT**

1 2 3 4 5

Ere **HALF** | my **DAYS** | in **THIS** | dark **WORLD** | and **WIDE**

 ISBN-978-81-8477-738-3

Mixed Metre with Iambic Feet

From *Intimations of Immortality*, by William Wordsworth

<table>
<tr><td>1 2 3 4 5
There WAS | a TIME | when MEAD | ow, GROVE, | and STREAM,</td><td>Iambic Pentameter</td></tr>
<tr><td>1 2 3 4
The EARTH, | and EV | ry COM | mon SIGHT,</td><td>Iambic Tetrameter</td></tr>
<tr><td>1 2
To ME | did SEEM</td><td>Iambic Dimeter</td></tr>
<tr><td>1 2 3 4
Ap PAR | elled IN | cel EST | ial LIGHT,</td><td>Iambic Tetrameter</td></tr>
<tr><td>1 2 3 4 5
The GLOR | y AND | the FRESH | ness OF | a DREAM.</td><td>Iambic Pentameter</td></tr>
<tr><td>1 2 3 4 5
It IS | not NOW | as IT | hath BEEN | of YORE;</td><td>Iambic Pentameter</td></tr>
<tr><td>1 2 3
Turn WHERE | so E'ER | I MAY,</td><td>Iambic Trimeter</td></tr>
<tr><td>1 2
By NIGHT | or DAY,</td><td>Iambic Dimeter</td></tr>
<tr><td>1 2 3 4 5 6
The THINGS | which I | have SEEN | I NOW | can SEE | no MORE.</td><td>Iambic Hexameter</td></tr>
</table>

Anapestic Tetrameter

From *The Destruction of Sennacherib*, by Lord George Gordon Byron

1 2 3 4
The As **SYR** | ian came **DOWN** | like the **WOLF** | on the **FOLD**,

1 2 3 4
And his **CO** | horts were **GLEAM** | ing in **PUR** | ple and **GOLD**;

1 2 3 4
And the **SHEEN** | of their **SPEARS** | was like **STARS** | on the **SEA**

 ISBN-978-81-8477-738-3

Trochaic Tetrameter

From *The Tyger*, by William Blake

1 2 3 4

TY ger | **TY** ger | **BURN** ning | **BRIGHT**

1 2 3 4

IN the | **FOR** ests | **OF** the | **NIGHT**

Level 3

5. Work with a partner. Tap out the rhythm of the remaining lines in the first verse of *Lady of Shalott*. What is the metre? Do you both agree?

6. Work with a partner. Refer to the above information and decide on the metre of the following lines. Do you agree with your findings? Write down your answer.

   Willows whiten, aspens quiver,
   Little breezes dusk and shiver
   Thro' the wave that runs for ever
   By the island in the river
   Flowing down to Camelot.

Vocabulary

Sound patterns and **rhythm** help the words in a poem to flow. Can you remember what assonance is? It is the repetition of vowel sounds. For example, in verse 1 Part 1 of *The Lady of Shalott*, the long vowel sound "o" is repeated:

That cl**o**the the w**o**ld and meet the sky;

Look at the following lines.

On either side the river lie
Long fields of barley and of rye,
That clothe the wold and meet the sky;

 ISBN-978-81-8477-738-3

As we read the lines, we can see how assonance also helps to create the sense that the barley and the rye are surrounding the "wold". Remember that sound effects can accentuate the poem's meaning.

A. There are numerous examples of assonance in the poem. Find some examples of assonance and an example of alliteration in the first three verses.

B. Read your examples to a partner and listen to the sounds and how the language flows. Discuss in what ways you think these sounds add to the meaning of the poem.

C. What letters create assonance in the following?

1. Dreams are made of sugar and cream.
2. With a needle and cotton she threaded the beads.
3. A calm summer sea charms everyone.

4. The frog turned into a handsome prince.
5. At night the white moon drifts.
6. A jumble of books and crumpled paper.
7. The schooner sails over open water.
8. The fledgling asleep in its nest.

 ISBN-978-81-8477-738-3

Grammar

The **hyphen** is used to create **compound words**. Over the time these hyphenated compounds may evolve into single words without a hyphen. For example:

tip-toe tiptoe

Some words can be spelled in several ways. For example:

water-ski waterski water ski

There are numerous examples of compound words in *The Lady of Shalott*, some of which were created by the poet for effect.

A. Find ten examples of compound words in *The Lady of Shalott*. Include three that have become single words today. Complete the table below.

Compound words	Have become single words (Indicate "yes" or "no")

 ISBN-978-81-8477-738-3

B. Create five compound words of your own that would suit the poem, *The Lady of Shalott*. Think about the natural surroundings, the boat and Camelot to create the words.

C. In the following sentences, fill in the blanks with compound words that mean the same as the underlined words. The compound words should all be written without hyphens.

1. A cage for keeping a bird in is a ____________________.
2. When the bus broke down, they had to call the ____________________ lorry to tow it to the garage.
3. We were in London when war broke out. We were in London at the ____________________ of war.
4. The government says it is going to have to cut back on spending. We're always hearing about ____________________s in government spending.

D. Choose two of your compound words and include them in a verse of your own.

E. How many compound words can you create from the following?

1. Create only full compound words without a hyphen.
2. Time yourself.

foot	day	light	shine	step
case	sun	moon	dream	over
with	cup	done	in	board
side	cut	man	under	snow
book	out	shelf	ball	

 ISBN-978-81-8477-738-3

F. Sometimes words are shortened for convenience. Write down the original word or words for the following. Make sure you spell them correctly!

1. ad
2. bike
3. blog
4. flu
5. fridge
6. hippo
7. mike
8. rhino

Listening

Listen carefully to the verse and answer the following questions.

1. What do these words mean?
    - ail
    - thee
    - loitering
    - sedge
2. In what condition is the knight? How do you know?
3. What person is the poem written in? What word tells you so?
4. What is the metre of this verse?
5. In what way does the style of this poem differ from that of *The Lady of Shalott*?

Speaking

In what sense is the Lady of Shalott a prisoner? Discuss this in your group.

1. Think about the following points to reach a conclusion.
    - Her life compared to the local people mentioned in the poem
    - How Lancelot appears to lead his life
    - Why the Lady of Shalott induces the curse and what she means when she says, "I am half sick of shadows"
2. Refer to the earlier work that you have done. Appoint a reporter to make notes. Share your notes with another group.

 ISBN-978-81-8477-738-3

Writing

A. Work with a partner. Tell each other the story of *The Lady of Shalott.*

- One of you should tell the first half, the other the second half.
- When you have finished, discuss whether or not you have left anything of importance out.
- On your own, write the story in prose form. Use one paragraph for each part of the poem.

B. Read the first two verses of *The Lady of Shalott* and follow the instructions.

- Tap out the rhythm.
- Note how the rhyme helps to push along the rhythm.
- Write a paragraph to explain why the poem is musical.

C. Work with a partner to write a narrative poem of your own.

- Think about the setting – will it take place in a ruined palace, a dense forest, an ancient castle or anywhere else?
- Work out the storyline together.
- Your poem should be a ghost or a mystery story.
- The poem does not have to rhyme, but it should include a repeating couplet.
- Think of some interesting images including similes and metaphors.
- You might even like to quote from *The Lady of Shalott*. For example, "The mirror crack'd from side to side." If you do, include your quote within quotation marks.

 ISBN-978-81-8477-738-3

Activity

Work in a group of three or four. You are required to produce information for a display on *The Lady of Shalott* and a famous Indian poem (or legend) of your own choice.

1. Think about the following before you begin.
   - a plan of the display
   - how you might advertise the display
   - the origins of the poems or stories and when they date from
   - commentary on the two works
   - what the works have in common, how they differ
   - illustrations
   - fact files

Other than the above elements, what else can you think of?

2. You will need to work as a team. How will you allot jobs and work together? List all the members of the group and their responsibilities in the table below.

Name	Responsibility

 ISBN-978-81-8477-738-3

6 Paper

Read the following excerpt from the story *Paper* by Catherine Lim.

1 He wanted it, he dreamed of it, he hankered after it. Once the notion of a big beautiful house had lodged itself in his imagination, Tay Soon nurtured it until it became the consuming passion of his life. A house. A dream house such as he had seen on his drives with his wife and children along the roads bordering the prestigious housing estates on the island, and in the glossy pages of *Homes and Modern Living*. Or rather, it was a house which was an amalgam of the best, the most beautiful aspects of the houses he had seen. He knew every detail of his dream house already, from the aluminium sliding doors to the actual shade of the dining-room carpet to the shape of the swimming pool. Kidney. He rather liked the shape. He was not ashamed of the enthusiasm with which he spoke of the dream house, an enthusiasm that belonged to women only, he was told. Indeed, his enthusiasm was so great that it had infected his wife and even his children, small though they were. Soon his wife, Yee Lian, was describing to her sister Yee Yeng, the dream house in all its perfection of shape and decor, and the children were telling their cousins and friends, "My daddy says that when our house is ready..."

2 They talked of the dream house endlessly. It had become a reality stronger than the reality of the small terraced house which they were sharing with Tay Soon's mother, to whom it belonged. Tay Soon's mother, whose little business of selling bottled curries and vegetable preserves which she made herself, left her little time for dreams, clucked her tongue and shook her head and made sarcastic remarks about the ambitiousness of young people nowadays.

3 "What's wrong with this house we're living in?" she added petulantly. "Aren't we all comfortable in it?"

 ISBN-978-81-8477-738-3

4 Not so long as you have your horrid ancestral altars all over the place, and your grotesque sense of colour – imagine painting the kitchen wall bright pink. But Yee Lian was tactful enough to keep the remarks to herself, or to make them only to her sister Yee Yeng, otherwise they were sure to reach the old lady, and there would be no end to her sharp tongue.

5 The house – the dream house – it would be a far cry from the little terraced house in which they were all living now, and Tay Soon and Yee Lian talked endlessly about it, and grew magnificently in their imaginations, this dream house of theirs with its timbered ceiling and panelled walls and sunken circular sitting-room which was to be carpeted in rich amber. It was no empty dream, for there was much money in the bank already. Forty thousand dollars had been saved. The house would cost many times that, but Tay Soon and Yee Lian with their good salaries would be able to manage very well. Once they took care of the down payment, they would be able to pay back monthly over a period of ten years – fifteen, twenty – what did it matter how long it took as along as the dream house was theirs? It had become the symbol of the peak of earthly achievement, and all of Tay Soon's energies and devotion were directed towards its realisation. His mother said, "You're a show-off, what's so grand about marble flooring and a swimming pool? Why don't you put your money to better use?" But the forty thousand grew steadily, and after Tay Soon and Yee Lian had put in every cent of their annual bonuses, it grew to forty-eight thousand, and husband and wife smiled at the smooth way their plans were growing.

 ISBN-978-81-8477-738-3

6 It was a time of growing interest in the stock market. The quotations for **stocks and shares** were climbing the charts, and the crowds in the rooms of the broking houses were growing perceptibly. "Might we not do something about this?" Yee Lian said to her husband. "Do you know that Dr Soo bought Rustan Banking for four dollars and today the shares are worth seven dollars each?" The temptation was great. The rewards were almost immediate. Thirty thousand dollars' worth of NBE (shares) became fifty-five thousand almost overnight.

Reading Comprehension

A. Answer the following questions.

Level 1

1. What kind of house did Tay Soon want?
2. Mention two qualities of Tay Soon's dream house described in paragraph 1.
3. Where did Tay Soon live and with whom was he staying?
4. Who else had become influenced by Tay Soon's desire for the dream house?
5. What was Tay Soon's mother's business?

Level 2

6. What do you think the dream house symbolised for Tay Soon?
7. Tay Soon referred to his desire for the house as "enthusiasm". What else might we call it?
8. What did Yee Lian think of her mother-in-law?

---

stocks and shares: the money (capital) a company raises through selling shares (equal parts) of the capital. Those owning shares are shareholders. The value of shares can increase or decrease on the stock market where shares are bought and sold.

 ISBN-978-81-8477-738-3

9. Why did Dr Soo interest Tay Soon and his wife?

10. Write a character study of Tay Soon. You can do this using the concept map below. Consider the following points.
    - His main character traits
    - His relationships and their nature
    - What others say about him
    - What he does / doesn't do

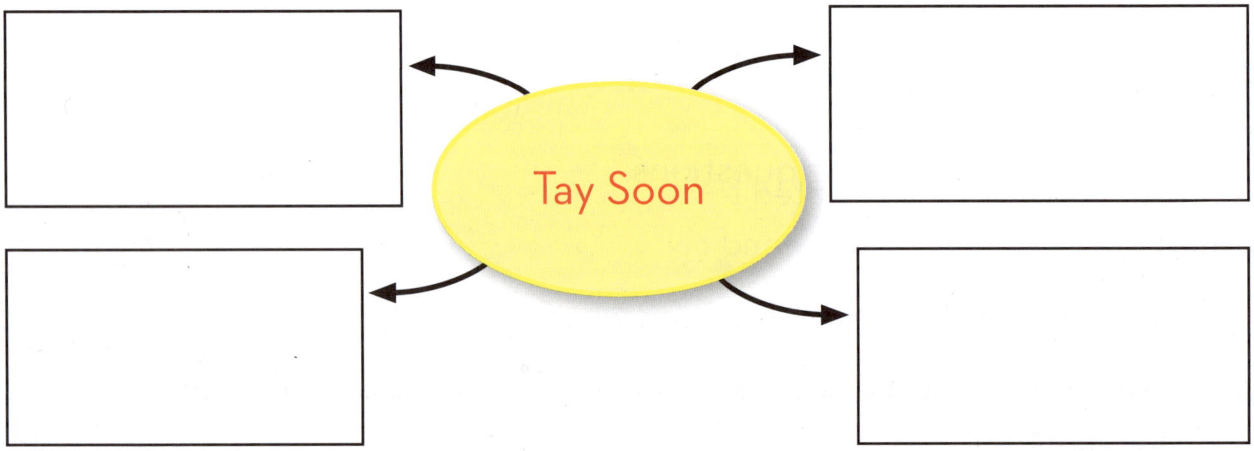

Remember you can add new arrows or further branches from the existing arrows.

B. Read the following note on first and third person narratives and answer the questions given after the break.

Level 3

Fiction is usually written in the third or first person.

In a first-person narrative, the narrator (or voice) is a character in the novel. By using the first person, you can reveal the character's thoughts and feelings more easily. However, you can only see events through the eyes of that character.

In a third-person narrative, you can see for yourself what all the characters are doing, because the narrative voice is not a character in the novel.

 ISBN-978-81-8477-738-3

11. What is *Paper* written in, first or third person? Underline the pronouns and proper nouns in the sentences below that tell you so.

> He wanted it, he dreamed of it, he hankered after it, as an addict after his opiate. Once the notion of a big beautiful house had lodged itself in his imagination, Tay Soon nurtured it until it became the consuming passion of his life.

12. Now, read it in the other person to a partner. Then discuss what you think the differences are between the two narrative voices. Make notes.

Vocabulary

There are several words related to money and finance in the excerpt from *Paper*. Look up the dictionary and check the given meaning of "stocks and shares". Check for the meanings of other words related to money and finance.

A. Look at the words listed below and explain what they mean as they are used in the text. Complete the table. Then check your answers with a partner and your teacher.

Words related to money and finance	Meaning
down payment	
pay back monthly	
annual bonuses	
stock market	
broking houses	

 ISBN-978-81-8477-738-3

B. In what way is the title *Paper* a metaphor? Think of more than one reason. (This will help you in thinking about why the author chose the title.)

C. Read the paragraphs and decide what the words in bold could mean and check your answers with a partner.

What is money? Put simply, any **legal tender** as payment.

Prior to the use of money people used **tokens** in exchange for goods or exchanged one thing directly for another such as apples for plums, or sacks of corn for a sheep. They would probably have **bartered** for goods.

We think people started using money about two and a half thousand years or so ago. Around this time people began to accept **coinage** in payment for goods or perhaps for services or work done. This meant that coins were given a **value**. They might also pay off **debts** with money, which was a more complicated activity. Indeed, the Babylonians who had a sophisticated civilization seemed to have had rules and **contracts** related to how **finance** should be carried out.

D. Together check your answers in a dictionary.

Bombay Stock Exchange

 ISBN-978-81-8477-738-3

E. Choose the matching words in the box with the definitions below. Write them in the space provided.

investment	quotation	salary	assets	interest
currency	shareholder	turnover	profit	capital

1. a fixed, regular, usually monthly payment for work done
2. a charge made for money that has been borrowed
3. money used to start up or run a business
4. a person who owns shares in a company
5. the current price of stocks and shares
6. the amount of money a person gains when they sell something for more than it cost them to buy it or produce it
7. a person's or company's total property
8. the system of money used in a country
9. money given or lent to a company in the hope of getting back a larger sum of money
10. the value of sales made by a business over a given period of time

F. Match the countries with the units of currency listed below. Write in the space provided.

Bangladesh	United States	Japan
Russia	Saudi Arabia	South Korea

1. Yen
2. Riyal
3. Rouble

 ISBN-978-81-8477-738-3

4. Taka
5. Won
6. Dollar

Grammar

An **adverbial phrase** is a phrase (a group of words) that acts like an adverb.

It answers questions such as "how", "who," "where", "when" and "why". Many adverbial phrases begin with a preposition. These are also called prepositional phrases. For example:

Tay Soon saved for his dream house **with enthusiasm**. (*How? With enthusiasm*)

Tay Soon saw the dream house **in his mind**. (*Where? In his mind*)

Sometimes, we could also use a single adverb. For example:

Tay soon saved for his dream house **enthusiastically**.

Remember

Prepositions are words such as: below, down, for, to, under, up, with.

 ISBN-978-81-8477-738-3

A. Complete the sentences given below by adding adverbs or adverbial phrases, and other suitable words. You should add adverbial phrases to at least three of the sentences.

1. Yee Lian told...
2. The dream house would be built...
3. Tay Soon's children...
4. Tay Soon planned...
5. Yee Yeng thought...
6. Tay Soon's mother...

B. Underline the adverbial phrases in the following sentences.

1. The man staggered to the side of the road and sat down on a stone.
2. She stared at me in amazement, then turned and walked towards the house.
3. If you push and I pull at the same time, we might manage to shift it into the garden.
4. I would ask you all to behave with restraint.

C. Replace the underlined adverbial phrases in the following sentences with adverbs that are equivalent in meaning.

For example:
They set to work <u>with enthusiasm</u>.
They set to work *enthusiastically*.

1. He looked at her <u>in triumph</u>.
2. They stared at the beggars <u>with suspicion</u>.
3. I'll deal with this matter <u>in person</u>.
4. The woman looked at the would-be robbers <u>with contempt</u>

 ISBN-978-81-8477-738-3

5. We do eat out in restaurants <u>on occasion</u>.

6. The boys walked <u>with care</u> across the muddy field.

7. The villagers watched <u>in fear</u> as smoke and ash rose from the mouth of the volcano.

8. Say nothing, but repeat the words over and over again <u>in your mind</u>.

D. What kind of adverbs or adverbial phrases are these? Are they adverbs (or adverbial phrases) of manner (how?), time (when?), place (where?), frequency (how often?) or duration (how long?)?

1. sympathetically
2. momentarily
3. by the bridge
4. once a week
5. here
6. yesterday
7. for a few seconds
8. three-weekly
9. recklessly
10. last Wednesday
11. almost always
12. on the path

E. Write five sentences using different adverbs or adverbial phrases from the above list. You may include more than one adverb or adverbial phrase in a sentence.

 ISBN-978-81-8477-738-3

Listening

Listen to the passage carefully for details and answer the following questions. The passage continues from the main excerpt above.

1. How much did they invest in the Far East Mart?
2. How many times had the shares in the Far East Mart increased in three days?
3. What did Tay Soon borrow to invest in OHTE? How much did it increase to in three days?
4. How much had they made in a few days?

Speaking

A. Work in a small group. Discuss what type of story you think *Paper* is, choosing from the list below.

1. a mystery story
2. a crime story
3. a cautionary tale
4. a thriller
5. a fantasy
6. a horror story

B. Come to an agreement amongst yourselves and discuss what details in the story suggest what type of story it will be and what you think might happen. Focus on the following points.

1. the characters' desires and dreams
2. what would make an interesting story

 ISBN-978-81-8477-738-3

Writing

Read the following excerpt from *Paper*.

> ... what did it matter how long it took as along as the dream house was theirs? It had become the symbol of the peak of earthly achievement, and all of Tay Soon's energies and devotion were directed towards its realisation. His mother said, "You're a show-off, what's so grand about marble flooring and a swimming pool? Why don't you put your money to better use?" But the forty thousand grew steadily, and after Tay Soon and Yee Lian had put in every cent of their annual bonuses, it grew to forty-eight thousand, and husband and wife smiled at the smooth way their plans were growing.

1. Answer the following questions.
   - What did Tay Soon and his wife value in life?
   - What did Tay Soon's mother value?
2. Make notes in the table below.
3. Find evidence in the text and add to the table.

Character	Attitude	Evidence
Tay Soon, Yee Lian		
Tay Soon's mother		

 ISBN-978-81-8477-738-3

4. Write an account (about 600 words) comparing what Tay Soon and Yee Lian valued with what Tay Soon's mother valued. Follow the guidelines below.
   - Look for information in the text.
   - Refer to details to support your point of view.
   - Refer to the work you have done earlier.
   - Conclude by saying which attitude you support and why.

Activity

Imagine the following scene.

A criminal is being followed by a detective through a city. The criminal turns corners, hides in shop doorways or in crowds, but the detective always picks up his trail. Eventually the criminal jumps onto a tram. What happens next? Does the criminal get away or not?

1. Write down the description in two different ways, choosing from the following narrative modes.
   - the first person
   - the second person
   - the third person
2. Read your description to a partner and vice versa. Which one do you like the best? Which one does your partner like best? Discuss why.

 ISBN-978-81-8477-738-3

Theme 4

Authors and Characters

A. What is happening in this picture? What do you think these people are doing?

B. Answer the following questions.

1. What do you think are the ingredients of a good story for young people?
2. What kind of stories do you prefer?
3. Are there any kinds of stories that you don't enjoy? Describe them.
4. What kind of characters do you find the most interesting? Why?
5. Do you think stories or novels should always have a happy ending?

 ISBN-978-81-8477-738-3

7 J. K. Rowling

Read the following passage by Scharada Dubey on renowned author J. K. Rowling.

1 "Please, please, don't let me fall to my death," pleaded the dark-haired girl. "Just hold on tight and let me climb back up. Please don't let me go! I'll fa-a-a-all!"

2 This last was said in such a theatrical wail that it brought their mother running to the spot from the garden where she had been peacefully reading in the shade of a tree.

3 "Joanne!" said their mother sharply. "How many times have I told you not to play that awfully silly game? Don't you realise how dangerous it can be?"

 ISBN-978-81-8477-738-3

4 Even as the first syllable of her name was leaving her mother's lips, the girl between the banisters had let go of her sister's arms. She fell, landing on her feet – the manner of her fall showing just how often both girls played their favourite "cliffhanger" game. The girls scurried to make themselves invisible from their visibly cross mother. They knew she was dreadfully angry – why else would she have called Jo by her full name, Joanne?

5 Joanne was born on 31 July 1965 in Gloucestershire, England. Her father, Peter James Rowling, and her mother, Anne Rowling, had both worked in the Royal Navy before settling down. Joanne was always called Jo by her parents and family, and was just short of her second birthday when her sister Dianne, who was always called Di, was born. The sisters were thus not only close in age, they were also extremely close in childhood – either fighting "like a pair of wildcats imprisoned together in a very small cage" as J. K. Rowling has described it, or sharing games and stories, friends and daring escapades.

6 Jo and Di spent a good part of their time together fighting, sometimes with dire results.

7 From the age of around three to the time she was nine, Joanne lived in Winterbourne, on the outskirts of Bristol. Here she went to a school that provided plenty of scope for crafts and creativity. As she recalls, "I enjoyed school in Winterbourne. It was a very relaxed environment; I remember lots of pottery-making, drawing and story-writing, which suited me perfectly." Very fond of making up stories to tell her sister, Joanne wrote her first "book" at the age of six. This was called "Rabbit" and featured a rabbit which gets sick with the measles and is visited by friends, including a giant bee called Miss Bee!

8 Around the time she was seven, Jo and her sister were friends with a brother and sister named Potter who lived on their street. This surname was later to be immortalised as Harry Potter's last name. While the real person, Ian Potter, who was Joanne's neighbour, bears no resemblance to Harry's character, there are other figures from her childhood who are said to inhabit her books, among them her elderly headmaster at St. Michael's Primary School, Alfred Dunn, who turns up in the Harry Potter books as Albus Dumbledore.

 ISBN-978-81-8477-738-3

9 Around Joanne's ninth birthday the family moved to Wales. It was around this time that Joanne lost a favourite grandparent, her paternal grandmother, Kathleen. Later in life, when her publishers felt that a book about a boy would not be appreciated by boy readers if it was by a female author, Joanne added the initial "K" to her name in honour of this grandmother, so that her name, J. K. Rowling, could be interpreted either as a man or woman writer.

10 Joanne moved to her secondary school when she was eleven. Here she made firm friends with Sean Harris, who owned a turquoise-and-white Ford Anglia. Zooming off into the darkness in Sean's car spelt a great deal of freedom to Joanne, since life in the countryside meant that transport was erratic and she often had to ask her father for a lift to wherever she wanted to go. Sean was special not only for being the first of Joanne's friends who learnt to drive a car, but also because he was the first person with whom she discussed her serious ambition to be a writer. He sincerely felt that Joanne would be a great success at it, and this meant a lot to her. She later dedicated the second Potter book, *The Chamber of Secrets*, to Sean and his car also features as the magic vehicle that takes Ron and Harry crashing into the Whomping Willow and finally disappears into the Enchanted Forest.

11 The darker themes of sadness and loss in the Harry Potter books undoubtedly have a lot to do with the fact that her mother was diagnosed with multiple sclerosis (MS), a crippling and degenerative disease of the central nervous system, when she was fifteen. Although it is possible for many people with MS to pursue a near-normal life with care, Joanne's mother's illness grew steadily worse after her diagnosis, and this cast a shadow over the whole family during her teenage years.

12 From the carefree roughhousing with her sister, to the deeper realisations brought about by her mother's illness and subsequent passing away, J. K. Rowling has captured a whole spectrum of action and emotion that particularly appeals to contemporary young readers.

 ISBN-978-81-8477-738-3

Reading Comprehension

Answer the following questions.

Level 1

1. What is J. K. Rowling's date and year of birth and where was she born?
2. Whom did she live with?
3. When her mother called her "Joanne" instead of "Jo", what did it indicate?
4. What story did J. K. Rowling write as a child? Mention a character in it apart from the main one.
5. What were the origins of Harry Potter's name?
6. What development had a profound effect on the young J. K. Rowling and how old was she at that time?
7. Name the characters and objects in J. K. Rowling's books that existed in real life.

Level 2

8. In what way does this biography of J. K. Rowling open as a story?
9. How can you tell that Joanne and her sister were close?
10. J. K. Rowling did not call herself Joanne Rowling (as she was known) but was advised to choose the name J. K. Rowling instead. Why was this change suggested and do you agree with it?
11. Who believed that J. K. Rowling could write stories and why do you think this was important?

 ISBN-978-81-8477-738-3

Level 3

12. Think of a dramatic incident in your own childhood and describe it as though it were the opening of a story. You can choose from the following.

    - The games you played as a small child
    - A dramatic event that involved the family
    - Something that happened on a holiday

    Can you think of anything else? Begin with dialogue as the text about J. K. Rowling does and use speech punctuation.

Vocabulary

There are many words in English that either sound the same but have different meanings, which are called **homonyms**, such as **bank**, or sound the same but are spelled differently and have different meanings, which are called **homophones**, such as **knew** and **new**.

A. Think of a word to go with each of these words from the passage *J. K. Rowling*. Write it down under "Matching word" and identify its type (homonym or homophone) under "Category".

Word	Matching word	Category
wail		
father		
pair		
dire		
time		

 ISBN-978-81-8477-738-3

bears		
felt		
spelt		
great		
tail		
rose		
minor		
aloud		
red		
whine		

B. Provide homophones for the following words. Sometimes there may be more than one example.

1. bizarre
2. buries
3. paws
4. sent
5. maze
6. taught

 ISBN-978-81-8477-738-3

C. Complete the following sentences by guessing the correct word that is also a homophone. Then write the other homophone underneath.

For example:
It was the end of summer and the drought had left the fields and meadows ___barren___.

homophone: baron

1. He slammed on the car ____________, swerved and pulled the vehicle to a halt.

   homophone:

2. The box contained everything except the small ____________ of string he was looking for.

   homophone:

3. Make sure you ____________ your name and details in the correct box on the left-hand side of the paper.

   homophone:

4. The prison ____________ had bare stone floor and a small barred window on one side of the room.

   homophone:

D. What are the meanings of the following homonyms? Write down the answer.

1. fine
2. light
3. pound
4. sole
5. trunk

E. Ask your partner to check the table. Do you agree with what your partner says?

 ISBN-978-81-8477-738-3

Grammar

A **noun phrase** is made up of a noun and some other words. It functions as a noun. For example:

the dark-haired girl

a very small cage

a favourite grandparent

Sometimes we use noun phrases to add clarity. For example:

my cat Lola

the writer J. K. Rowling

her sister Dianne

A. Underline the noun phrases in the following sentences.

1. Your very first task is to gather up all the dirty clothes that are lying on the floor and put them in the laundry basket.
2. We have patients in this hospital with very interesting diseases, you know.
3. Whose daughter is that blonde-haired little girl over there beside the garden gate?
4. They have invited some well-known film star, whose name I have forgotten, to hand out the prizes.
5. The surgeons inserted a three-inch steel pin into his left leg.

B. Write your own sentences using the six examples given above.

C. Add two more sentences using your own noun phrases.

 ISBN-978-81-8477-738-3

D. Underline the longest noun phrase in each of the following sentences.

1. He gulped down the delicious soup.
2. The young trees are thriving.
3. He told an entertaining story.
4. The willow branches shook.
5. The traffic lane was congested.

E. Use the following noun phrases in your own sentences.

1. a challenging puzzle
2. a well-known actor
3. the great bear
4. the latest gadget
5. a new skateboard

Listening

Listen to the text about J. K. Rowling and answer the questions below.

1. What was J. K. Rowling's job before she became a writer and where did she work?
2. Why did she live in Edinburgh?
3. What did J. K. Rowling use to write her novel?
4. Where did she write her novel? Why?
5. Which publisher finally accepted the novel?

 ISBN-978-81-8477-738-3

Speaking

Carry out a group discussion. Each member of the group should talk about who or what has influenced their ideas and behaviour. (For example, they may have a grandparent or elderly relative who has given them good advice.)

1. Take a few minutes to think about your talk before you begin.
2. When a member has given their talk, the other members can ask questions.
3. As a group create some ground rules before you begin. The following are some examples:
   - Agree on how many minutes you will allow someone to speak for.
   - No one should speak when another person is giving their talk.
   - You have to raise your hand if you wish to comment.

Writing

Write a short autobiography.

Consider including the following points.

1. important events in a timeline starting from your birth
2. an early memory (such as beginning your first school)
3. special occasions or things that are important to you
4. your hopes for the future

 ISBN-978-81-8477-738-3

Activity

Work with a partner to carry out some role play.

1. One of you should take the part of J. K. Rowling (the interviewee) and the other should take the part of a television interviewer.
2. You should carry out an imaginary interview.
3. Before you begin, the interviewer should list a series of questions (about twelve) to ask the interviewee. Following are some pointers about framing the questions.
    - These should be mainly open questions, with some closed ones.
    - Your questions should be mainly based on the information in the text *J. K. Rowling*.
    - You may include questions that involve general aspects of the Harry Potter books, providing that your interviewee is familiar with them.
    - You should also be prepared to change your questions as you go along, for example, if the interviewee says something that gives you a new idea.
4. The interviewee should read *J. K. Rowling* again and become familiar with the information.
    - You should try to remember general information about the Harry Potter books.
    - You should also try to give a detailed answer, particularly to those open questions that ask you to describe your feelings.

Remember

An **open question** has no precise answer. It asks the interviewee about their feelings. For example:

How did you feel when you won?

A **closed question** has a precise answer. For example:

When is your birthday?

 ISBN-978-81-8477-738-3

8 Tom Sawyer

Read the following excerpt from *The Adventures of Tom Sawyer* by Mark Twain.

1 She went to the open door and stood in it, and looked out among the tomato vines and "**jimpson**" weeds that constituted the garden. No Tom. So she lifted up her voice, at an angle calculated for distance, and shouted:

2 "Y-o-u-u- *Tom*!"

3 There was a slight noise behind her, and she turned just in time to seize a small boy by the slack of his **roundabout** and arrest his flight. "There! I might have thought of that closer. What you been doing in there?"

4 "Nothing."

5 "Nothing! Look at your hands, and look at your mouth. What is that **truck?**"

---

jimpson: a bushy weed
roundabout: short jacket
truck: mess or rubbish

 ISBN-978-81-8477-738-3

6 "I don't know, Aunt."

7 "Well, I know. It's jam, that's what it is. Forty times I've said if you didn't let that jam alone I'd skin you. Hand me that switch."

8 The switch hovered in the air. The peril was desperate.

9 "My! Look behind you, Aunt!"

10 The old lady whirled around and snatched her skirts out of danger, and the lad fled, on the instant, scrambled up the high board fence, and disappeared over it. His Aunt Polly stood surprised a moment, and then broke into a gentle laugh.

11 "Hang the boy, can't I ever learn anything? Ain't he played me tricks enough like that for me to be looking out for him by this time? But old fools is the biggest fools there is. Can't learn an old dog new tricks, as the saying is..."

Reading Comprehension

A. Answer the following questions.

Level 1

1. What plants are in the garden?
2. Who is Aunt Polly?
3. Can you estimate her age?
4. Why is Aunt Polly cross?
5. What do you think the switch could be?

Level 2

6. What clues tell you the story is set in the country rather than the city?
7. How does Tom trick Aunt Polly?

 ISBN-978-81-8477-738-3

8. Think of three adjectives to describe Tom.

9. Do you think Aunt Polly would have beaten Tom? Why or why not?

Level 3

B. Read the following note on "characterisation" and answer the questions.

Writers can reveal a character by *showing* what they are doing, and by *telling* the reader through the narrative voice. Most good stories include both, but usually there is more "showing" than "telling".

"Telling" is referred to as direct characterisation, "showing" as indirect characterisation.

Look at **A** and **B** below:

A **"showing": we see what the character is wearing through her actions**

The old lady whirled around and snatched her skirts...

B **"telling": the narrative voice is telling the reader what the old lady is wearing**

The old lady wore several skirts.

10. Add two more sentences to **A** that will help to reveal the old lady's appearance as you see it. Use indirect characterisation.

11. Now do the same to **B** using direct characterisation.

12. Which do you think is more vivid, direct or indirect characterisation, and why? Write a sentence to explain.

 ISBN-978-81-8477-738-3

13. Read the text given below.

"Tom!"

No answer.

"Tom!"

No answer.

"What's gone with that boy, I wonder? You Tom!"

The old lady pulled her spectacles down and looked over them, about the room; then she put them up and looked out under them.

What does it suggest about Tom and Aunt Polly. Write your remarks in the boxes.

Tom	Aunt Polly

14. Write an imaginary dialogue between Tom and Aunt Polly in which Tom appears to be behaving himself. Think about how Aunt Polly would react. Would she be pleased? Would she be suspicious? Use speech punctuation correctly.

Vocabulary

There are some **expressions** or **sayings** in the excerpt from *The Adventure of Tom Sawyer* which are still used in contemporary American and British English such as "**skin you**", "**scrambled up**" etc. However, there are also certain expressions which have become archaic and are no longer in use such as "**the peril was desparate**".

A. Look at the sayings in the table and find them in the excerpt.

1. Work out what they mean from the context.
2. Decide whether they are still used or archaic.

 ISBN-978-81-8477-738-3

3. Decide if they are American English only.

Saying	Meaning	Archaic?	American English only?
the slack of his roundabout			
I'd skin you			
on the instant			
hang the boy			
can't learn any old dog new tricks			
what is that truck			

B. Can you guess the meaning of the following expressions? Add them to your table.

1. playing hookey
2. mighty smart
3. make fun (of him or her)
4. in a twinkling

C. Write down the archaic words from the following list. Also, guess and write their meanings.

britches	pencil	companion	surprise	colossal	beforetime
window	alack	forthwith	oak	calculator	fringe
hark	document	methinks	fan	rooftop	motorbike
wallpaper	verily	suitcase	silver	betwixt	anthology
polite	ocean	shallows	erelong	nigh	scientist

 ISBN-978-81-8477-738-3

D. Can you guess what the following expressions mean? Take it in turns to explain to a partner.

1. dashed decent!
2. gosh!
3. beside oneself
4. jolly dee!
5. all ears
6. purse-proud
7. haul over the coals
8. kick up a dust

Grammar . Punctuation

If we **quote** from a passage we also use quotation marks. For example:

Aunt Polly is often suspicious of Tom and frequently seems both **"perplexed"** and **"surprised"** by him.

Remember, you should try to imbed your quotes in the sentence – make them part of the sentence.

A. Write a short commentary (about three sentences) about Tom in which you quote from the excerpt to support what you say. Use quotation marks correctly.

 ISBN-978-81-8477-738-3

B. The passage below is about a famous book *The Railway Children* that has never been out of print. It was written by Edith Nesbit (1858–1924). Where do you think quotation marks should be used? There are three places. Write out the phrases correctly using single quotation marks.

The Railway Children tells the story of three young people, Roberta, Bobbie for short, Peter, and Phyllis, who lead a normal life with loving parents. Their mother likes to read to them and make up poetry at special times such as the christening of new kittens or the refurnishing of the doll's house. Their father is a good man, never cross, never unjust and always ready for a game. However the pretty life in Edgecombe Villa comes to an abrupt end. Their father is accused of a crime he did not commit.

Listening

Listen to this text about Mark Twain and answer the following questions.

Mark Twain

1. What was Mark Twain's real name?
2. When was he born and when did he die? How old was he at the time of his death?

 ISBN-978-81-8477-738-3

3. What work did he do before he became a writer?
4. Which is considered his greatest book?
5. What is *The Prince and the Pauper* about?

Speaking

Carry out a discussion with a partner or in a small group of no more than three.

1. *The Adventures of Tom Sawyer* was published in 1876. Discuss in what ways Tom:
   - is similar to children today.
   - is different from children today.
2. Appoint a member of the group to make notes.
3. Appoint another member of the group to report back to another group.

Writing

A. Apart from being annoyed, how else does Tom make Aunt Polly feel? Look back at the work you have done and also find evidence (a quotation from the excerpt) and complete the table below.

Evidence (What Aunt Polly says/thinks about Tom)	What does this tell you about Aunt Polly

B. Use your work to write a commentary of how Aunt Polly feels about Tom. Remember that she feels more than one way about him.

Activity

Characters are central to any story and are usually affected by their circumstances and what happens to them, but they can also make things happen, which affects the events. By the end of the novel, characters, particularly the main character, have mostly changed or learned something about life. Authors not only create characters, they develop them throughout the novel.

A. Create your own mischievous child character. The character must do something that affects others in some way. You may keep in mind the following points while sketching the character. You can also use points of your own.

1. They find something of value but tell no one about it.
2. They run away from home.
3. They play a trick that backfires.

B. Use a spider diagram similar to the one below to make notes about your character. Give your character a name.

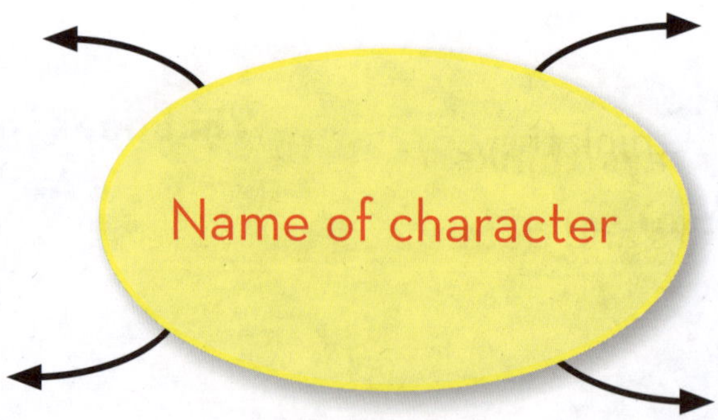

C. Write a short story drawing on the information from your diagram. Remember, you can introduce other characters (but not too many) and change the plot as you write.

 ISBN-978-81-8477-738-3

Theme 5

Myths

Look at the above picture carefully and answer the following questions.

1. Do you think that the figures in it are real? Why or why not?
2. What are the figures doing?
3. What world do you think they come from?
4. Describe the colours and details used by the artist.

 ISBN-978-81-8477-738-3

9 Two Myths about Fire

Read the following passage on two myths about fire as told by Sharada Bhanu, Padma Malini Raghavan and Padma Seshadri.

1 The Titans, according to Greek mythology, were a race of gods sprung from the earth and sky. Prometheus was a Titan, the son of Iapetus and Asia. His name means "forethought" and his brother's name, Epimetheus, means "afterthought".

2 Prometheus fashioned the race of men out of clay. His brother had the task of distributing various qualities and abilities among the animals. Prometheus wanted to make his creation special. So he gave man technology with the help of the goddess Athena and he gave fire taken from the god Hephaestus. He educated man on how to use fire to work metals. In fact, the growth of civilisation depends on how skillfully man controls and uses fire.

3 Prometheus offered the god Zeus a sacrifice. He wanted men to have the good meat. So he made two piles of offerings. One pile had the good meat and this he covered over with the entrails of the animal. The second pile had all the bones and this he covered over with fat. He asked Zeus to choose and he chose the one with a lot of fat on it. On discovering the trick, Zeus was enraged and took away fire from man to spite Prometheus. Not to be outwitted so easily, Prometheus stole the embers and hid them inside a fennel stalk and brought it to man. (Interestingly, dry fennel makes excellent kindling and is useful to start a fire.)

4 Prometheus suffered a terrible punishment. He was chained to Mount Causasus in Scythia, with a stake through his middle. During the day a giant eagle ate his liver and entrails. At night, the organs grew again. The next morning the eagle was back to feed. Prometheus endured this for many centuries until Hercules came there and killed the eagle to set him free.

 ISBN-978-81-8477-738-3

5 In Persian belief, fire is the last and most important of the creations by Ahura Mazda, the wise lord. Along with wisdom, Ahura Mazda is associated with light and brightness. His arch opponent is Ahriman or Angra Mainyu who lives in absolute darkness.

6 Before creation, there was emptiness and void between them. Then Ahura Mazda decided he would start his act of creation. First he created the sky, bright and shining. Then he created water, pure and clear. Third on the wise lord's list was the earth, flat and round. It was flat in a very literal sense – there were no mountains or valleys. Earth had a level surface, signifying there were no inequalities. Then the wise lord created plants that were moist and sweet and supple too because of the moisture. They had no rough bark. Next came the animals, big and small. Then he created the First Man, Gayamard, handsome and bright. Now we come to the important point of our story. Sky, Water, Earth, Plants and Animals were created before Man was created. Fire was created after First Man came, to fulfil his special needs. Ahura Mazda distributed fire to all and ordered it to serve mankind both for cooking and for keeping warm.

7 How Angra Mainyu attacked Ahura Mazda's seven creations by bringing darkness to the sky, bitterness to water, uneven hills and valleys to the earth, thorns to the plants, thoughts of violence to animals, sickness and death to man and smoke to the fire, and how Ahura Mazda created the Seven Bounteous Immortals to protect his seven creations are part of the **Zoroastrian** story of creation.

8 When a **Jashan ceremony** is enacted in the Zoroastrian place of worship, it is a thanksgiving for the perfect harmony in which Ahura Mazda placed his seven creations, a state we shall reclaim some day. But fire is remembered everyday as the embodiment of the Creator, who is radiant and luminous. It stands for spiritual light. That is why the Zoroastrian place of worship is called a Fire Temple – celebrating Ahura Mazda's special gift for man.

Zoroastrian: a believer in the prophet Zoroaster and the creator Ahura Mazda and the destroyer Ahriman

Jashan ceremony: a Zoroastrian ceremony; "Jashan" means "worship ceremony"

 ISBN-978-81-8477-738-3

Reading Comprehension

Answer the following questions.

Level 1

1. To which mythology do the Titans belong? How were they created?
2. Who was Prometheus? What does his name mean?
3. Who do you think Zeus was? What power did he have over Prometheus?
4. Who were Ahura Mazda and Ahriman?
5. What was the first man according to Persian belief called? What was he like?

Level 2

6. Why do you think "the growth of civilisation depends on how skillfully man controls and uses fire"? Explain by referring to an example.
7. How can you tell that Prometheus was fearless? Mention an example, without going into too much detail.
8. How can you tell that humans are beneath the gods in importance in these myths?
9. What were Ahura Mazda's seven creations and what did they signify?
10. Why is fire important to Zoroastrians?

Level 3

11. What was Prometheus like? Do you think that he was brave or hotheaded, or both?
    - Think of adjectives to describe him and list them.
    - Create a spider diagram of his main features, describing the following.
        i. His physical appearance
        ii. His nature

 ISBN-978-81-8477-738-3

12. Write a character study of Prometheus. Use the concept map below, considering the following points.

    1. His main character traits
    2. His relationships and their nature
    3. What he does / doesn't do
    4. The consequences of his choices

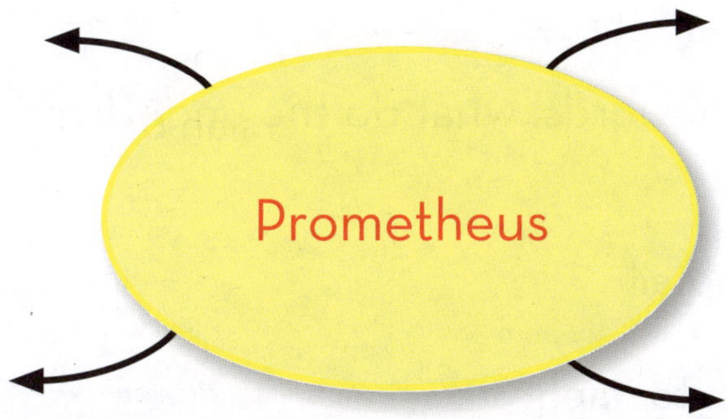

Remember that you can add new arrows or further branches from the existing arrows.

Vocabulary

A. Using a dictionary, wherever necessary, answer the following questions.

1. If a film star has had a meteoric rise to fame, how quickly have they become famous?
2. If you saw someone with a lugubrious expression on their face, would they be looking happy or sad?
3. What can a kleptomaniac not stop doing?

 ISBN-978-81-8477-738-3

4. What are vertebrates and why do they have this name?

5. If someone had an insatiable appetite, would they eat a lot of food or only a little?

B. Look at the pairs of words in the following examples.

- triangle and tricycle
- triennial, trilogy or tripod

  Here "tri" means three.

In the following pair of words, what do the underlined part of the words mean?

1. monologue, monorail
2. autobiography, autograph
3. multicoloured, multinational
4. polygamy, polygon
5. telescope, television
6. biology, biopsy
7. antipollution, anticrime
8. microbe, microscope
9. panorama, pandemic
10. thermometer, thermostat

 ISBN-978-81-8477-738-3

C. Do you know the meaning of the words in the table below? If not, find out the meanings, even with the help of the dictionary.

Word	My definition	Dictionary definition
fennel		
mythology		
entrails		
Titan		
embers		
void		
embodiment		
supple		
literal		
luminous		

 ISBN-978-81-8477-738-3

1. Complete the column "My definition" and check your answers with a partner.
2. Then complete the column "Dictionary definition". You will need a dictionary to do this activity.
3. Compare your definitions with those from the dictionary. How close are they?

D. Do you know the definition of the following words, which have something to do with myth, without using a dictionary? Write down your answers.

1. supernatural
2. folklore
3. heroine
4. custom
5. culture
6. legend
7. ancient
8. mortal
9. immortality
10. enchanted

E. Work with a partner to check your answers in question 1 using a dictionary.

 ISBN-978-81-8477-738-3

Grammar

The subject and the verb in a sentence have to agree. This is called **verb agreement**. If the subject is singular, you need a singular verb. If it is plural, you need a plural verb. For example:

singular subject → **He** / singular verb → **was**	singular subject → **The Titan** / singular verb → **was**
He was a god.	**The Titan was** a god.
plural subject → **They** / plural verb → **were**	plural subject → **The Titans** / plural verb → **were**
They were gods.	**The Titans were** gods.

A collective noun can have a singular or plural verb depending on how it is used in a sentence. For example:

The audience was spellbound as the Greek tragedy reached its climax.

The audience were clapping their hands in time to the music.

A. In some of these sentences the subject and verb agree. Find those sentences in which they do not agree and correct them.

1. The belief in the power of the gods is common in Ancient Greece.
2. Prometheus were a Titan who came before Zeus in Greek mythology.
3. Prometheus's brother were responsible for giving the animals their qualities.
4. In the myth, Prometheus ask Zeus to choose between good and bad meat.

 ISBN-978-81-8477-738-3

5. Zeus become very angry with Prometheus and punishes him cruelly.
6. Another name for Ahriman, Ahura Mazda's arch-enemy, are Angra Mainyu.
7. In Persia, Ahura Mazda's creations are celebrated at a thanksgiving ceremony.

B. Pick out the verbs in the following conversation which do not correctly agree with their subjects and rewrite the conversation with all the verbs in the correct form.

Sanjiv: Would you like a cup of coffee, Rajesh?

Rajesh: No, thanks. Coffee and tea doesn't agree with me.

Sanjiv: Coffee with a little milk and three spoonfuls of sugar is what I like.

Rajesh: Three spoonfuls of sugar! That seem an awful lot of sugar!

Sanjiv: That's nothing! My father takes four spoonfuls! My father and mother both likes a lot of sugar.

Rajesh: If you take too much sugar, your teeth rots. My dentist say so. What do it say about sugar in your encyclopaedia?

Sanjiv: I don't know. I hasn't looked to see. If it do say that sugar are bad for your teeth, my parents and I should certainly cut down on the amount we take.

C. The verb agreement is wrong in some of the following sentences. Find those that do not agree and correct them.

1. Tom has bought a new pair of trainers and several sweaters.
2. When we has finished the meal we'll go to the movies.
3. They has no way of getting here without avoiding the traffic in the town.
4. Lily haven't remembered to take her lunch with her.
5. Have you remembered to feed the cat?
6. Every Wednesday afternoon they has to take their kit for the games.
7. I hasn't got enough money to buy the photographic equipment I need.

 ISBN-978-81-8477-738-3

8. The humming bird have beautiful wings with shimmering colours.
9. Several of the students have been playing in chess competitions.
10. Bhakti has to play the guitar each evening before her evening meal.

Listening

Listen to the text and answer the following questions.

1. Where do creatures in myths usually live?
2. In what important way are gods different from humans?
3. What does a sphinx look like?
4. Name another supernatural being mentioned in the text. What does it look like?
5. What is the explanation for why myths exist?
6. Can you identify the mythical creature in the picture? What is his significance in Greek mythology?

Speaking

A. Work in a small group of no more than four. Give a talk on any one of the following topics.

1. How Prometheus tricked Zeus
2. The punishment Prometheus suffered
3. How Ahura Mazda carried out his act of creation
4. How Ahriman attacked Ahura Mazda's creation

 ISBN-978-81-8477-738-3

B. Each one in your group should choose a different topic.

C. Before you begin, refer back to the work that you have already done to help you in this exercise.

Writing

Write your own myth. Include the following features and characters.

1. a description of the setting
2. a god or goddess that can change into other creatures
3. a villain (human or a god)
4. fire and other natural elements (such as water or thunder)
5. humans responding or dealing with what happens

Activity

Read the following note on myth.

Myths are often packed with detail. They usually include many events and characters. One story sometimes leads into another or is linked to it in some way through a character. Myths are therefore often told as a series. For example:

- Sanskrit epics
- Chinese myths
- myths of Ancient Greece
- Norse myths
- Celtic myths
- Roman myths
- Persian myths
- Native American myths

 ISBN-978-81-8477-738-3

Now, choose one topic from the above list and carry out your own research on it. Some pointers are provided here for your help.

1. You do not have to retell the myths, although you can mention some characters and some of their stories.
2. On the basis of your research, work on the following.
    - a fact file
    - a timeline (or identify important dates where you can)
    - information about the series as a whole
    - illustrations to highlight the stories
3. Redraft your work for others to read.

 ISBN-978-81-8477-738-3

10 Ancient Myths

Read the following excerpt from *Heaven and Earth and Man* by Cyril Birch.

1 One day the goddess Nü-kua, whose body was that of a dragon but whose head was of a human form, grew weary of the loneliness of earth. After long thought she stooped and took from the ground a huge lump of clay. From this she fashioned with her dragon claws a tiny creature. The head she shaped after the pattern of her own, but to the body she gave two arms and two legs. She set the little thing back on the ground and the first human being came to life and danced and made sounds of joy to delight the eyes and ears of the goddess. Quickly she made many more of these charming humans, and felt lonely no longer as they danced together all about her.

2 Then, as she rested a while from her task and watched the sons and daughters of her own creation go off together across the earth, a new thought came to her. What would become of the world when all the humans she had made grew old and died? They were fine beings well fitted to rule over the beasts of the earth; but they would not live forever. To fill the earth with humans when these had gone to make more to take their place would mean an endless task for the goddess. And so to solve this problem Nü-kua brought together man and woman and taught them the ways of marriage. Now they would create for themselves their own sons and daughters, and these in turn could continue to people the earth throughout time.

3 After this gift of marriage from Nü-kua, further blessings came to man from her husband, the great god Fu-hsi. He again had a human head but the body of a dragon. He taught men how to weave ropes to make nets for fishing, and he made the lute from which men first drew music. His also was the priceless gift of fire. Men had seen and feared the fire, which was struck from the forest trees by the passing of the Lord of the

 ISBN-978-81-8477-738-3

Thunderstorm. But Fu-hsi, who was the son of this same lord, taught men to drill wood against wood and make fire for their own use, for warmth and cooking.

4 Already the creatures of Nü-kua's making could speak their thoughts to one another, but Fu-hsi now drew for them the eight precious symbols with which they could begin to make records for those who were to come after. He drew three strokes ☰ to represent Heaven; the three strokes broken ☷ represented earth. That symbol whose middle stroke was solid ☵ represented water, that whose middle stroke was broken ☲ represented fire. A solid stroke above ☶ gave the sign for mountains, a solid stroke beneath ☳ the sign for storm; a broken line below ☴ showed wind, a broken line on top ☱ showed marshland. With these eight powerful symbols man could begin to record all he observed of the world about him.

5 For long years men lived their lives in a world of peace. Then, suddenly, there spread from Heaven to earth a conflict that threatened to put an end to all creation. This was the battle between the Spirit of Water, Kung-kung, and the Spirit of Fire, Chu-jung. Down to earth came the turbulent, wilful Kung-kung to whip up huge waves on river and lake and lead his scaly hordes against his arch-enemy, Fire. Chu-jung fought back with tongues of flame and scorching breath and halted the rebel Water in his path. Kung-kung's armies dispersed and he, their leader, turned and fled. But his flight brought with it a peril greater yet. For, dashing blindly off to the west, Kung-kung struck his head against the mountain Pu-chou-shan, which was none other than the pillar that in the western corner held up the sky.

6 Kung-kung made good his escape, but he left the world in a disastrous state. Great holes appeared in the sky, whilst the earth tilted up in the west. In that region great cracks and fissures appeared which are still to be seen to this day. All the rivers and lakes spilled out their waters, which ran off and still run eastwards: off to the south-east, where the earth had slipped down low and ran the waters together to form a

 ISBN-978-81-8477-738-3

vast ocean there. Meanwhile out of the shaken mountain forests fire still raged forth, and wild beasts of every kind left their lairs to maraud through the world of helpless, terrified men.

Reading Comprehension

A. Answer the following questions.

Level 1

1. Who was Nü-kua? Without giving too many details, describe her appearance.
2. What did she make and why?
3. Who was Nü-kua's husband and what did he look like?
4. What priceless gift did he give to humans? Why?
5. What did the eight powerful symbols allow humans to do?
6. Who were Kung-kung and Chu-jung?
7. What was Pu-chou-shan?

Level 2

8. Early people did not know that humans developed through a process of evolution. The myth offers a way of explaining human development and behaviour. Now, (a) scan the text to find other explanations for natural events and human behaviour and (b) design a table, with a heading and sub-headings, and make notes of what you have found.
9. What do you understand by the phrase "chaos and order"? Refer to a dictionary if you need to and write a sentence to explain the phrase. In what way is chaos and order depicted in the myth?

 ISBN-978-81-8477-738-3

B. Read the note on sequence of a narrative and answer the questions given below.

The plot or storyline of a narrative tells us what happens. What we often think of as the "beginning, middle and end" usually follows a chronological sequence or time order. However, we can also think of the organisational pattern in a more sophisticated way, which is as follows:

Introduction: the beginning in which the characters and setting are usually presented

↓

Complication: when a problem (or unusual event) occurs that moves towards the "crisis"

↓

Crisis: sometimes called "the climax" when a highpoint or very dramatic moment occurs and which usually leads to the "resolution"

↓

Resolution: when the solution to the problem occurs, though not necessarily happily

 ISBN-978-81-8477-738-3

Level 3

10. Work out the organisational pattern of *Ancient Myths* by identifying the following.
    - introduction
    - complication
    - crisis
11. What do you think the resolution of the story will be?
12. Think of a simple story that you know, such as a myth or folktale, or create your own plot, and complete the table below. Two starting sentences are given for your help.

Introduction	A woodland goddess lived in a dark forest...
Problem	One day she found...
Crisis	
Resolution	

Vocabulary

A. Scan *Ancient Myths* for the following vocabulary. Then circle the most appropriate meaning for each word, as it is used in the excerpt.

Vocabulary	Meanings
1. fashioned	shaped / corrected
2. charming	glamorous / appealing
3. beings	humans / animals
4. people	travel / populate
5. drew	sketched / extracted
6. maraud	plunder / invade

 ISBN-978-81-8477-738-3

B. Many words in English have more than one meaning. Read the following sentences and then select from the words in brackets, the one which most closely matches the meaning of the underlined word, as it is used in the sentence.

1. I <u>gather</u> you're leaving tomorrow morning. (recollect / understand)
2. There's a good <u>chance</u> that they'll win a gold medal. (probability / risk)
3. Our <u>plan</u> was to split up and search in all the gardens and parks. (intention / layout)
4. His skin condition was <u>aggravated</u> by being out in the hot sun. (annoyed / worsened)
5. The company finds itself in a very difficult financial <u>situation</u> right now. (location / circumstances)
6. There must be a <u>fault</u> in the wiring somewhere. (blame / defect)
7. Many of our soldiers have received <u>decorations</u> for bravery. (medals / ornaments)
8. The children made a <u>vain</u> attempt to tidy up their rooms before their parents came home. (proud / unsuccessful)

C. Describe the differences in the meanings of the underlined words in the following sentences.

1. Those books are my <u>property</u>.

   State two <u>properties</u> of hydrogen.

2. The problem seems to be <u>insoluble</u>.

   Sand is <u>insoluble</u> in water.

 ISBN-978-81-8477-738-3

3. Leave the parcels on the <u>table</u> over there.
   Add up the figures in each column of the <u>table</u>.

4. He came home from school with a good <u>report</u>.
   The shell burst with a loud <u>report</u>.

5. The university hopes to <u>forge</u> closer links with the local community.
   The signature on the cheque has clearly been <u>forged</u>.

D. Write down two meanings (or more) of the following words.

1. address
2. balloon
3. block
4. drain
5. license
6. matter
7. notch
8. paddle
9. roll
10. slide

 ISBN-978-81-8477-738-3

Grammar

A **simple sentence** has only one main clause. For example:

Nü-kua made clay figures.

A **compound sentence** has two main clauses, joined together by a conjunction such as "and", "but", "or" and "so". For example:

main clause | main clause

Nü-kua made clay figures and **they kept her company**.

A **complex sentence** has a main clause and a subordinate clause. A subordinate clause cannot stand alone. For example:

main clause | subordinate clause

Nü-kua made clay figures because she was lonely.

A. Expand the following simple sentences into compound sentences.

1. Nü-kua loved her humans.
2. The humans danced together.
3. Fu-hsi weaved rope.
4. He created a lute.
5. He gave the gift of fire.

B. State if the following are main clauses or subordinate clauses.

1. Dogs bark.
2. The thunder clapped.
3. That is red and blue.
4. While he was waiting.
5. When the sun comes out.

 ISBN-978-81-8477-738-3

6. That's the entrance.
7. Since he left for the city.
8. After the local cinema closes.
9. It's raining!
10. I love playing tennis.

C. Do the following sentences have one main clause or two?

1. He cleaned the kitchen and he swept the path.
2. Dev did not arrive on time because his train was late.
3. Shut the door!
4. Shall we stay in or shall we go out?
5. How long does it take to drive to Mumbai?
6. I know but she knows better.
7. It was bright and sunny so we went for a walk.
8. Can anyone mend this computer?

 ISBN-978-81-8477-738-3

D. Add a main clause to each of these subordinate clauses to form a complex sentence.

1. Before Kung-kung whipped up the waves...
2. While Chu-jung fought back...
3. As Kung-kung fled...
4. As the waters ran together...
5. ...when things fell apart.

Listening

Listen carefully to the resolution of *Ancient Myths* and answer the following questions.

1. Who brought back order into the world?
2. What were the stones used for?
3. Where were the stones from?
4. Why was the giant turtle killed?
5. How was the world different from before? List the changes in the table below.

Before	After

 ISBN-978-81-8477-738-3

Speaking

Choose a myth from any culture that you know (or find out one) and present a talk to a group about it.

1. You can either:
    - tell the myth as a story, or
    - describe its important characters and features, and explain where it comes from.
2. You should not read your speech aloud, but become familiar with what you are going to say.

Writing

Read the following note on Fretag's pyramid.

A timeline can show when the major events occur in a story. You can also depict it in such a way that:

- it shows the build-up to the crisis point
- problems make way for a solution

This is called the **Fretag's pyramid** after Gustav Freytag, who invented it.

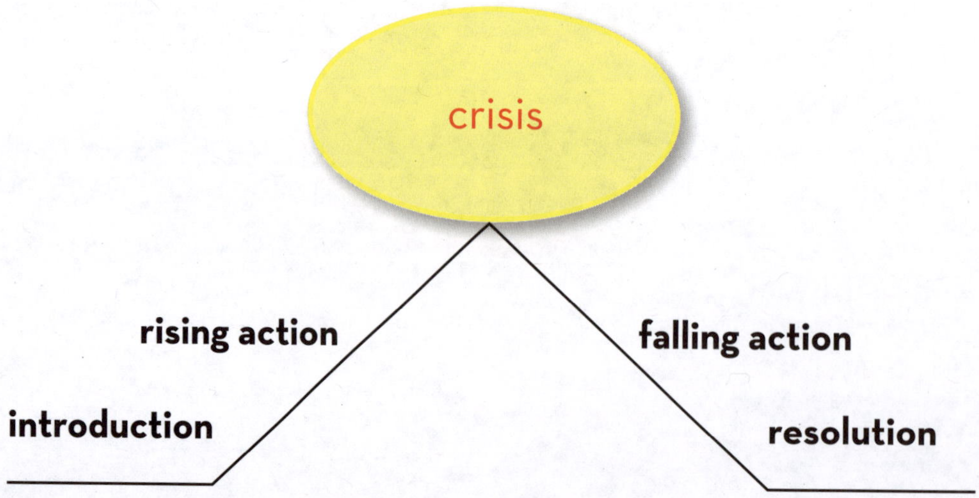

 ISBN-978-81-8477-738-3

Now use Freytag's pyramid to plan a story of your own, using the following prompts.

1. two young people (give them names and some detail)
2. an ancient ruin
3. a winged horse

Activity

Work in a group of three. Read each other's story plans that you wrote under "Writing".

1. Between you identify the strengths and weaknesses of each plan, thinking about the plot, ideas and characters.
2. Decide which is the best plan and why.
3. Then appoint a note maker and complete the following writing frame.

Group:	Date:
We chose (name of student and plan) ______________ as the best for several reasons.	
We thought that the....	
Also, we thought that...	

 ISBN-978-81-8477-738-3

In addition...

However, we also thought that the other plans had good points too. For example...

We also thought...

But overall we chose (name of student and plan) ________________________ mainly because...

 ISBN-978-81-8477-738-3

Theme 6

Health

A. Look at the above picture.

1. What place is this?
2. Describe what you can see in the picture.

B. Answer the following questions.

1. What are your favourite dishes?
2. Do you know the ingredients of your favourite food? What are they?
3. Are your favourite dishes good for you?
4. Name two dishes that are good for you. Do you know why?
5. Can you name any spices?

 ISBN-978-81-8477-738-3

11 Overcoming Polio

Read the following passage by Mary Green.

1 Polio or poliomyelitis is an infectious disease, caused by a virus. For many people there are no symptoms and they develop immunity to the disease. The body has a defense system (the immune system) that responds to the virus by creating antibodies that attack the virus.

2 The body's immune system is generally very effective. When a virus or bacteria enters the body, the body's alarm system is set off and antibodies spring into action. They search for the virus or bacteria cells. Antibodies find the invading cells because they are different from the body's own cells. They either kill the cells or prevent them from working properly so that they become ineffective and unable to cause harm. When all the virus cells have been destroyed, the immune system then clears the dead cells from the body.

3 However, in some cases of polio, the immune system is not able to kill the virus and the infection runs its course. This can result in death or in serious long-lasting problems, such as paralysis or problems with the muscles. Children are often at risk and the disease is most common in areas where there is poor sanitation and lack of availability of clean water. If children are suffering from malnutrition, their immune systems may not work well. So, plenty of good food is also important to fend off the disease.

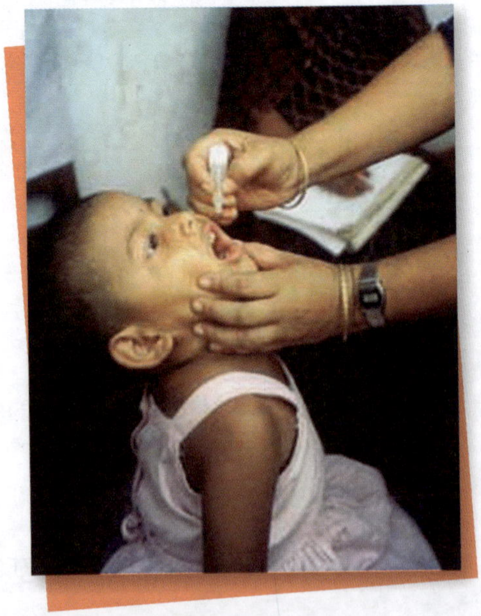

 ISBN-978-81-8477-738-3

4 Till the time a vaccine was developed, polio was widespread across the world. It was also widely present in India but steps have been taken to deal with it. The object was to completely remove it, and the disease has now almost died out. This is a great triumph and was possible largely due to a vaccination programme and a huge budget of almost $2.5 billion.

5 The approach towards dealing with an outbreak is also important. Quick action is needed. If an outbreak occurs, nurses and doctors must be sent to that area at the earliest. Good quality, up-to-date vaccines to deal with particular strains of the disease must also be used. Then the number of cases will decrease. Alongside this, it is important to continue improvements in sanitation and hygiene.

If no cases are reported for three years, a country is considered to be free of the disease.

Reading Comprehension

Answer the following questions.

Level 1

1. What causes poliomyelitis?
2. How does the body generally respond to the infection?
3. If someone contracts polio, what might happen?
4. Where is the disease most common?
5. What stopped the occurrence of polio?

Level 2

6. Why do some people not contract polio?
7. Why might it be difficult to eliminate polio in a community?

 ISBN-978-81-8477-738-3

8. Which members of the community are most at risk from contracting polio and how do you think this can affect their future?

9. What do you think are the main reasons behind India overcoming polio to a large extent? Think of three reasons.

Level 3

10. Find the paragraph that tells you how the body's immune system deals with viruses or bacteria. Create a vertical flow diagram (like the one given below) that explains how the immune system works.

    - Add as many boxes as you think is necessary.
    - Your comments in the flow diagram should sum up the main points from the paragraph.
    - Make sure your sentences are not too long. Be concise.

How the immune system deals with infection.

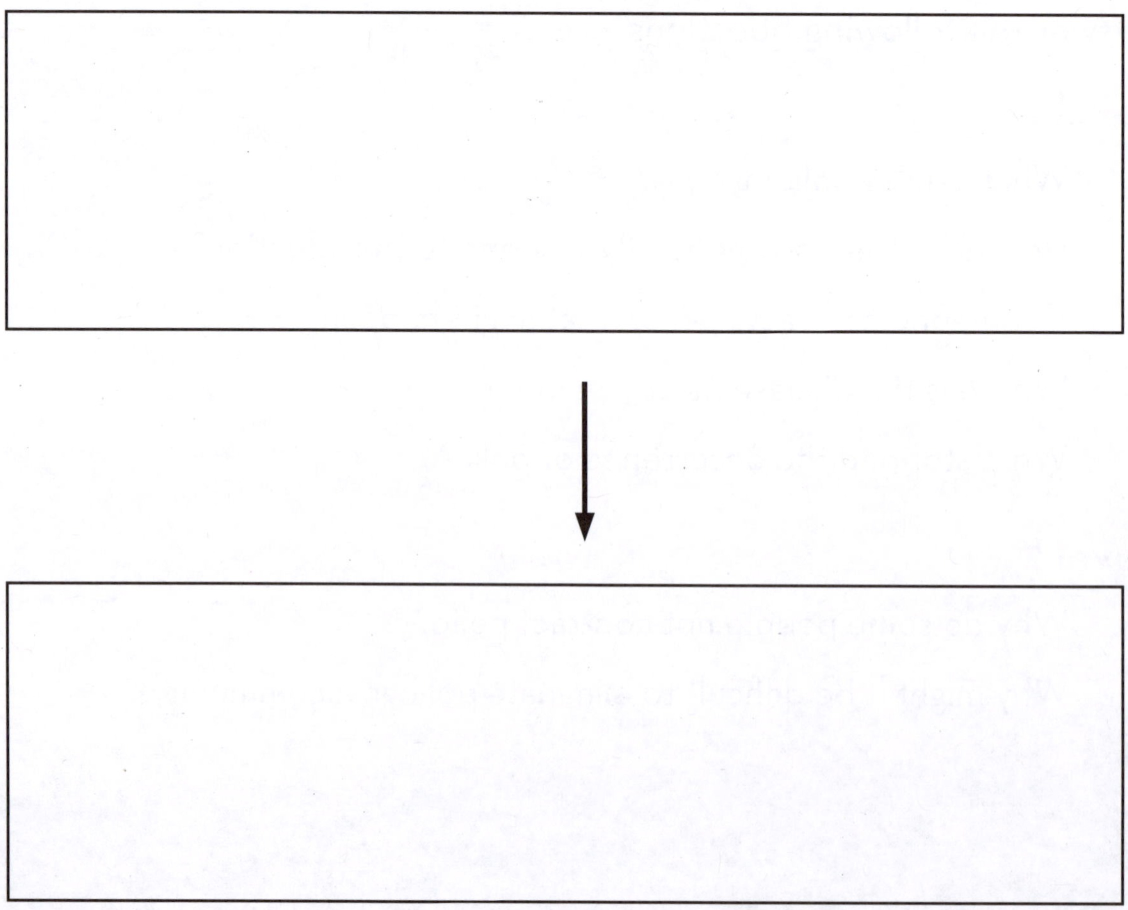

 ISBN-978-81-8477-738-3

Vocabulary

Like other technical words in English, many of the terms related to health and medicine have their origin in the Greek or Latin. For example, allergy is derived from the Greek word *allos* meaning "other different or strange". Similarly, the word gland traces its roots to the Latin word *glandula* meaning "gland of the throat, tonsil".

A. The following words related to medicine and health have their origins in either the Greek or Latin languages. Match the words to their original meanings.

Vocabulary	Original meanings
poliomyelitis	free
immunity	healthy
antibodies	cow
virus	stick or rod
bacteria	bad, nourish
sanitation	grey, marrow, inflammation
vaccine	against
malnutrition	poison

 ISBN-978-81-8477-738-3

B. Check the vocabulary's origins in a dictionary and see whether or not you were correct.

C. In the table above, add "Greek" or "Latin" to show which language the terms came from.

D. Choose the matching words in the box with the definitions below.

prescription	aspirin	bandage	amputation	germ

1. A medicine taken to relieve pain and reduce fever.
2. A virus or bacterium that causes disease.
3. A doctor's instructions about the medicine to be given to a patient.
4. A strip of cloth that is wound round a part of your body to cover a wound.
5. The cutting off of all or some part of a person's arm or leg for medical reasons.

E. Find words with the following Greek *prefixes*. Check their meaning in a dictionary.

1. auto-
2. bio-
3. geo-
4. hydro-
5. micro-
6. philo-

 ISBN-978-81-8477-738-3

F. Find words with the following Latin *suffixes*. Check their meaning in a dictionary.

1. -able
2. -ible
3. -ic
4. -ity
5. -ous
6. -ure

G. Use a dictionary to find the meaning of the following words. Are they Greek or Latin in origin? Write down the answer. Time yourself.

1. fastidious
2. gastric
3. horticulture
4. indigo
5. mediate
6. ostentation
7. Palaeontology
8. rhetoric

 ISBN-978-81-8477-738-3

Grammar

Homographs are words that have the same spelling but are not pronounced in the same way and have different grammatical usage. For example:

noun

The **object** is to completely remove polio.

verb

"I strongly **object** to your methods!" he said loudly.

Also notice how the noun "object" is pronounced differently from the verb "object":

stress — noun: **ob**ject

stress — verb: ob**ject**

A. Write two sentences for each homograph in the box to show its different usage.

conflict	contract	reject	subject

- Indicate whether the word is a noun or a verb in each of the sentences.
- Underline where the stress occurs in the word.

B. Can you think of a third meaning for the word "object"? What is it, a noun or a verb? Where does the stress come?

 ISBN-978-81-8477-738-3

C. See the concept map below. Make a similar map for another homograph.

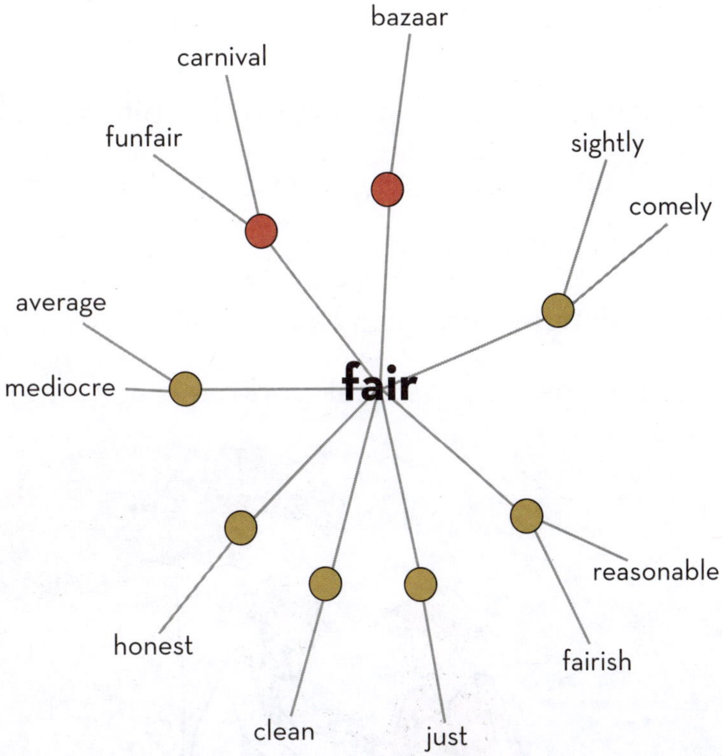

D. Look at the words in bold print. Where does the stress come in these words?

1. I will **record** the information in the log-book.
2. There is very little public **transport** between her and the next village.
3. They grew a range of **produce** in the small garden.
4. He likes to **rebel**, so he won't do anything I ask him to do.
5. Do you think they will **convict** him of the crime?
6. She is doing a **project** on Sri Lanka in school.

E. In the above sentences, which of them are nouns and which verbs? Write down the answers.

 ISBN-978-81-8477-738-3

Listening

Listen to the passage and answer the following questions.

1. Why is it difficult for rural people to get to hospitals?
2. Where does the barefoot doctor get his / her name from?
3. What is a barefoot doctor's job?
4. Name a common ailment in rural areas.
5. How has technology helped medical workers reach rural areas?

Speaking

Work with a partner. Give a talk to another pair about the kinds of things you would expect a mobile health team to do.

1. Include the following points:
   - what kind of health workers would be in the team
   - what kind of vehicle would be required
   - what they would need to carry
   - who is most likely to need care

 ISBN-978-81-8477-738-3

2. You will also need to work out how to present the talk. Note down your speaking points.

Notes

3. Evaluate how well you did with the pair you presented your talk to, especially regarding content and presentation.

Writing

A. Carry out some research on the Internet with your teacher's guidance and find out about one of the following.

1. smallpox and how it was overcome
2. the mosquito and our health
3. conserving water in Tamil Nadu

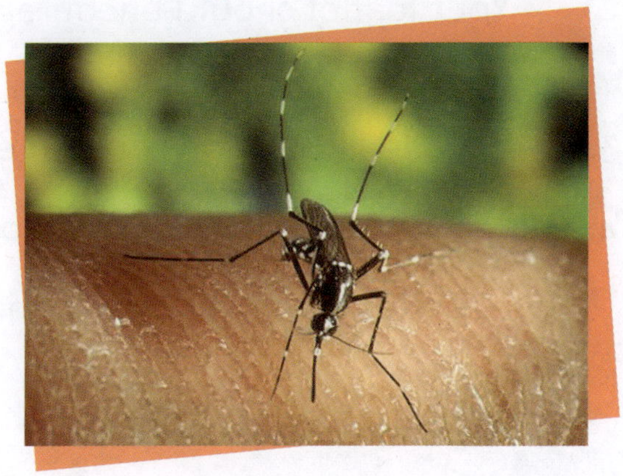

B. Write an article for a newspaper or a Web page, discussing the topic you have chosen.

1. Set your points out clearly in paragraphs.
2. Use suitable connectors. (For example, "As well as" to give additional information; "Finally" to sequence your points and "However" to qualify a point.)

Activity

Design a one-page leaflet about good hygiene.

1. Focus on the following:
    - hand hygiene
    - hygiene in the kitchen
    - washing shared household linens (such as towels)
    - first-aid hygiene at home or in school
    - hygiene for not spreading infections (such as a cold)
    - disinfectants.
2. Your leaflet should encourage people to practise good hygiene. So, it should be user-friendly.
3. Include illustrations and an eye-catching presentation.
4. Think of a saying or make up a compound word as a memory prompt.

    For example, "hygiene for health" or "kitchen-clean".

 ISBN-978-81-8477-738-3

12 Healthy Eating for Teens

Read the following passage.

1 Eating well is often hard for teens. Hanging around with friends, frequenting fast food outlets and snacking can lead to excessive intake of fat, sugar and calories and insufficient intake of important vitamins and minerals. Adolescence is a time of increased nutrient needs. During the rapid growth of puberty, the body has increased need for calories and key nutrients including protein, calcium, iron, folate and zinc. Iron and calcium are particularly important nutrients for your body during adolescence.

2 Iron helps your blood carry oxygen to all your muscles. It helps your brain function and your immune system fight disease. Choosing iron-rich food sources can help keep your body working optimally.

3 Your body will actually absorb more calcium from the foods you eat during puberty. The increased need for skeletal growth signals your body to "grab" all the calcium it can. The problem is most adolescents simply are not eating enough calcium-rich food to meet their needs. If you do not meet your calcium needs during this critical time when your bones are growing, you may end up with weaker bones that are more prone to fractures.

4 Experts estimate that for every 5 per cent increase in adolescent bone mass, there is a 40 per cent decrease in the risk of bone fractures later in life. There is a limited time window to deposit calcium into bone. Bones grow and incorporate calcium rapidly during teen years. By the time you reach your early twenties, however, calcium is no longer added to bone. Worse yet, when you get a little older, you actually start losing calcium from your bones. Currently most teen girls are getting far less than the recommended 700 milligrams of calcium per day. So, reach for foods rich in calcium now.

 ISBN-978-81-8477-738-3

Healthy Diet Basics

5 There are healthy eating tips that can help you develop food habits that promote good health. Learning to eat well now can help lower your risk of developing disease in the future. Here is a chart you can use to help ensure you're meeting key nutrient needs. Nutrient needs are best met by choosing a variety of different foods. Vitamin and mineral supplements cannot replace a healthy diet and can be harmful if used inappropriately. Talk to your doctor before taking any nutritional supplements. The following recommended servings probably will not provide all of your energy (calorie) needs, but you can afford to add a few higher fat foods or some sweet treats if most of your selections come from these nutrient-dense food groups.

 ISBN-978-81-8477-738-3

Food group	Servings per day	What a serving equals
Calcium-rich foods	3-4	1 cup of low-fat milk, milk pudding or yoghurt 1.5 oz. cheese 1 cup of calcium-fortified soy beverage
Protein foods	2-3	3 oz. portion of meat, fish or chicken 3 eggs 3 oz. tofu 4 tablespoons peanut butter 1/2 cup cooked beans (soya, chickpeas, lentils, etc.) *Choose lean meat, poultry without skin and vegetarian protein sources to limit artery-clogging saturated fats.
Rice and alternatives	6-7	1/2 bowl rice 2 slices of bread 1 cup pasta or noodles 2 small chapatti 1 bread bun, pau or bagel 3/4 cup ready-to-eat cereal 4 biscuits *Choose whole grain sources to enrich your fibre intake.

 ISBN-978-81-8477-738-3

Food group	Servings per day	What a serving equals
Vegetables	2–3	1/2 cup cooked leafy vegetables 1 cup cooked non-leafy vegetables 1 raw carrot 1 1/2 cup salad greens 1/2 cup vegetable juice *Choose a good variety of vegetable. Leafy greens are great sources of folate; orange and yellow-orange veggies provide beta-carotene.
Fruit	2–3	1 slice papaya, melon, pineapple, watermelon, etc. 1 cup cut-up fruit 1/2 cup 100% fruit juice 1/2 cup canned fruit (juice-packed) *Pick citrus fruits to boost vitamin C intake. Eat a variety of fruits to boost the cancer-fighting agents.

(Source: www.nutrition.com.sg)

Reading Comprehension

Answer the following questions.

Level 1

1. Why do teenagers often find it hard to eat well?
2. What are the key nutrients that young people need?
3. Why do young people need increased nutrients?
4. What does iron do?
5. What can happen if young people do not have enough calcium?

 ISBN-978-81-8477-738-3

Level 2

6. Do you agree that eating well is difficult for the young? Give reason for your answer.
7. Why can't you make up the loss of bone mass later in life if you have insufficient calcium when you are young? Mention two reasons.
8. From reading the article, what kind of food do you think you should avoid or only eat a little of?
9. Why do you think it is important to develop healthy eating habits when you are young?

Level 3

10. Create a healthy lunch menu for teenagers.
    - Scan the food table above for useful information to include.
    - Set out your menu attractively and include at least two dishes that will appeal to young people.
    - Remember to create a balanced diet.
    - Also refer to the food table to create some nourishing drinks.

Vocabulary

Some English words sound very similar and are often confused. These words are called **malapropisms**. They are named after a comic character Mrs Malaprop from the play *The Rivals* (1775) by Richard Brinsley Sheridan. Mrs Malaprop continually muddles her words. (Her name comes from "malapropos" which means "unsuitable".) For example, she says:

"He can tell you the **perpendiculars**." *(She means "**particulars**".)*

or

"He is the very **pineapple** of politeness." *(She means "**pinnacle**".)*

 ISBN-978-81-8477-738-3

A. Find the malapropisms in the following sentences and correct them.

1. He had an access of fat and sugar in his diet.
2. For optional health make sure you eat enough fruit and vegetables.
3. There are many important nutriments that you need.
4. Dedicated coconut and coconut milk is used in several recipes.
5. A series attitude to good health is the first step on the healthy route.
6. We all need to except that exercise is important to good health.
7. I have litter affluence over my cat's behaviour.
8. Do you know the saying "A rolling stone gathers no moths"?
9. My father used a fire distinguisher to put out the kitchen fire.
10. Don't is a contraption of do not.

B. Make up your own sentences using malapropisms from the list below. Use a dictionary if you need to.

	Actual word	Malapropism
1.	community	immunity
2.	delicious	suspicious
3.	comprehend	reprehend
4.	banished	bandaged
5.	alligator	allegory
6.	sceptic	septic
7.	smidgen	pigeon
8.	twister	twitcher

 ISBN-978-81-8477-738-3

Grammar

Ordering sentences in different ways makes a paragraph more interesting. For example, the first sentence of the text *Healthy Eating for Teens* begins with a verbal noun "Eating". It is a verb in its "ing" form and "Eating" acts as a noun. A verbal noun is sometimes called a **gerund**.

verbal noun (gerund)

Eating well is often hard for teens.

We could rewrite the above, without changing its meaning, using the infinitive "to eat":

infinitive

It is hard for teens **to eat** well.

A. Find the verbal nouns in this paragraph. Then add three sentences of your own. Include some verbal nouns.

His cooking is excellent. He made a wonderful raita and naan the other day that went well with a delicious vegetable curry. Mixing the ingredients the night before made the preparation easy, or so he said. Shopping for the right food would be difficult enough. Eating the meal was much better.

 ISBN-978-81-8477-738-3

B. Can you remember how to use the imperative? If not, check the examples in Unit 1. Find three different imperatives in the food group chart.

C. The following sentences are written using the infinitive. Rewrite them so that they use a verbal noun.

1. It isn't easy to whistle.
2. It's crucial to keep quiet at the right moment.
3. It's popular to tap dance.
4. It won't do to make a fuss.
5. To sing is supposed to be good for your health.

D. Complete the following sentences using a verbal noun of your own.

1. ____________ is his favourite sport.
2. ____________ and speaking are two important skills.
3. We both try to make sure that ____________ takes place regularly.
4. ____________ and ____________ are popular with many people.
5. ____________ the young swallows took to the air was fantastic!

Remember

When we use the imperative, the second person "you" is dropped.

Listening

Listen to this passage about spices and answer the questions.

1. Where do spices come from?
2. Where do herbs come from?

 ISBN-978-81-8477-738-3

3. What cuisines use many spices?

4. What spices are mentioned?

5. What part of the body are spices supposed to be particularly good for?

Speaking

A. What can you remember about healthy food? Without checking, speak to a partner for two minutes about how to eat healthily.

B. Your partner should then present a two-minute talk to you on spices and their value.

Writing

A. Read the information below on spices used in both Indian dishes and other global cuisines, and complete the exercises given below.

1. Scan the information to find the following.

- what each spice looks like
- how the spice is used
- the possible health benefits of each spice

 ISBN-978-81-8477-738-3

2. If there are any words you do not fully understand, check them in a dictionary.

3. Present all the information as a diagram of your own design. Remember, the reader must be able to scan the diagram to find information quickly.

4. To see how quickly information can be found on your diagram, write five questions about the information and give them to a partner to answer. Time it and see how long it takes them. You should also answer questions about your partner's diagram.

5. Discuss together how you can improve your diagrams.

Spices

Turmeric – This orange-coloured powder, which comes from the root of the plant, is common in Asia and used in a range of curries and traditional Persian dishes. In Europe, it was once known as Indian Saffron. It is generally considered to aid digestion and may be helpful in the prevention of cancer.

Coriander – The fine, flimsy leaves of this plant are widely used in cooking across the world and are well known in Indian food. The seeds are also used. The herb helps to preserve food because it acts against bacteria. It is also considered to aid digestion and be good for healthy blood. However, some people are allergic to coriander.

Cumin – This plant belongs to the parsley group and is found in Asia and the Mediterranean regions. The seeds are used in cooking and are present in many curry-based dishes as well as soups and some Dutch cheeses. It contains iron.

Chilli – Chilli can be dried or crushed and is used across the world to give a tang to dishes. It can be very hot to the taste. It is sometimes blended with cumin and garlic. It may benefit the heart, but chilli should be used sparingly and not consumed too often.

 ISBN-978-81-8477-738-3

Ginger – Ginger has long been used as a medicine, since it is supposed to be anti-inflammatory and to aid digestion. The root of the plant is used in many Asian and Caribbean dishes. Ginger cake, ginger tea and ginger beer are also popular across the world.

Garlic – Garlic is really a vegetable related to the onion, but it is often grouped with spices and used with spices in recipes. It is probably the most common ingredient in a range of cuisines, whether in Asia or Europe or the Americas. For best results garlic cloves are crushed and added to dishes. Numerous claims have been made for garlic's health benefits, such as being good for the heart, helping to fight cancer, or overcoming infections. Whether or not this is the case, different cultures have used it as a medicine for hundreds of years. It is high in vitamin C.

B. Find or write a recipe for a healthy main meal. Include some spices. Set out your recipe appropriately using the imperative.

Activity

Put together an information leaflet (of six pages or more) for young people about healthy eating, focusing on the following points.

1. the skills you have learned
2. the work you have done so far
3. additional information from further research

You may use the following steps to help you put together your leaflet.

Research and planning

- Make a rough first draft of your ideas for your leaflet.
- Decide what you want to include and carry out your research.

 ISBN-978-81-8477-738-3

- Then decide on the following.
  (i) the layout of your leaflet (See "Presenting information" below)
  (ii) what information you may need to cut or add
- Revise your draft in the light of what you have found out.

Points to consider

- what a balanced diet means
- the kinds of food you should eat
- what is *not* healthy eating
- the recipe you created
- the menu you created
- your diagram about spices
- tips for daily eating

Presenting information

- Think about your teenage audience. What will appeal to them? Why will they want to read your leaflet?
- When will you write in sentences and paragraphs and when will it be best to use bullet points?
- What headings and subheadings are appropriate?
- What typeface and colours will you use?

 ISBN-978-81-8477-738-3